BE PREPARED
A COMPREHENSIVE GUIDE
TO COLLEGE PLANNING

DR. ROBERT MCCLERREN

Everything you need to know from
ADMISSIONS to VOCABULARY

BALBOA.
PRESS
A DIVISION OF HAY HOUSE

Balboa Press books may be ordered through booksellers or by contacting:

Balboa Press
A Division of Hay House
1663 Liberty Drive
Bloomington, IN 47403
www.balboapress.com
1 (877) 407-4847

Because of the dynamic nature of the Internet, any web addresses or links contained in this book may have changed since publication and may no longer be valid. The views expressed in this work are solely those of the author and do not necessarily reflect the views of the publisher, and the publisher hereby disclaims any responsibility for them.

The author of this book does not dispense medical advice or prescribe the use of any technique as a form of treatment for physical, emotional, or medical problems without the advice of a physician, either directly or indirectly. The intent of the author is only to offer information of a general nature to help you in your quest for emotional and spiritual well-being. In the event you use any of the information in this book for yourself, which is your constitutional right, the author and the publisher assume no responsibility for your actions.

Any people depicted in stock imagery provided by Thinkstock are models, and such images are being used for illustrative purposes only.
Certain stock imagery © Thinkstock.

Print information available on the last page.

ISBN: 978-1-5043-8177-2 (sc)
ISBN: 978-1-5043-8178-9 (e)

Library of Congress Control Number: 2017909081

Balboa Press rev. date: 07/26/2017

TABLE OF CONTENTS

Section 1

Earning a College Degree

Section 2

Non-Degree Options

FOREWORD

The purpose of this book is all about "forward", as in thinking forward. Planning, questioning, organizing, researching, goal-setting, and in general looking forward are not skills or tools made obsolete by technology, no matter what my college students claim. As an adjunct English instructor since 1974 I have seen many improvements in technology's assistance for adults who seek to grow into a variety of careers and enhance or retrain themselves to keep pace with the evolution of their fields of study. Regardless of technology, however, preparedness is necessary for the human factor. It does not hinder creativity; instead, it releases time to enhance creativity.

Competition is key in searching for a job, scholarship, college entrance, pay raise, promotion within a career, training for a specialty within a field. What separates one from other applicants? Preparedness.

Kay Allard

Adjunct Faculty
English Composition
College of DuPage
Glen Ellyn, IL

Section 1

EARNING A COLLEGE DEGREE

FINDING THE BEST COLLEGE

Which college is the best college? Occasional through the years I have been asked what is the best college. That's a question that cannot be properly answered until you find what the individuals idea of "best" is.

- Proximity (the closest commute is the "best" for me) (The closest to family is "best" for me)
- Lowest tuition (The least I have to spend the better)
- Highest tuition (Things that are "best" cost the most)
- Majors offered (The "best" has unusual or hard to find majors)
- Small (The "best" is small, intimate school, where I can become known by faculty and staff)
- Mega School (The bigger the better means I will identify with a well known school)
- A State school (Identifies me with my home state) (Identifies me with their athletic teams)
- A private school (Known for it's exclusivity and selective acceptance)
- A school of notoriety (Known to be the alma matter of famous accomplished people)
- Academics (Known for exceptional scholarship)

If you were eligible, and cost was not an issue, it might be your choice to attend a prestigious Ivy League school for your college education. Since that may not be an option, how do you decide which college is best? After notoriety, what's next?

Choose The Right Type Of School For Your Educational Goals

- Community College

- Private School
- State University
- Trade School

Level of study

Certificates – Associates – Bachelors – Masters – Doctorate

Many colleges will offer a degree you are looking for. The suitability of a school can depend on many important factors.

DECIDING FACTORS

- Academic Program
- Location
- Tuition
- Admissions
- Testing
- Accreditation
- Semesters Vs. Quarters
- Credit By Exam
- Transferability
- Credit For Military Training
- GI Bill
- Tuition Assistance
- Prior Learning Assessment

If all other factors being equal when it comes to employment opportunities, who would most likely have the advantage over being hired or promoted; a College graduate or someone with no additional training past High School?

Who needs College?

- Those whose career path requires a college degree
- Those whose career path will benefit from a certificate completion program

Genius without education is like silver in the mine.
Benjamin Franklin

DO YOUR OWN HOMEWORK

After careful review, you should be able to easily find schools with programs that match your educational & career goals.

GET THE INFORMATION YOU NEED TO SUCCEED

Using the information contained in these pages, will enable your to select the school and program that is right for you.

Don't rely on web sites that can give you the run around leaving important questions unanswered. Beware. Many sites are primarily a sales pitch to attend a pre-determined school. They redirect you to a college that is sponsoring the search: luring students into programs with "Featured Universities." Other sites are design to funnel the masses into a one size fits all training program. Forget about time consuming searches on websites that only provide general information. They limit their recommendations to a few select schools. You can take a more comprehensive approach. VetsGuide maintains a database on over 1800 SOC member Colleges. Go to http://www.vetsguide.com/servicemembers-opportunity-colleges.html and click the school name to see its profile.

After researching information within these pages, you will be more prepared to make the best possible choice for schools and your future. You will then enjoy the benefit of a customized & unbiased educational plan.

CHOOSING YOUR FIELD OF STUDY

If you are still in the process of deciding on a major, there are tools that can indicate what career fields are suited toward your talents, skills, personality and way of thinking.

The DISC Profile

An assessment and theory that sheds light on how we think, act, and interact with other people especially when it comes to decision-making and leadership.

www.thediscpersonalitytest.com

Myers-Briggs Type Indicator

A questionnaire designed to indicate personality types. There are 4 dichotomies resulting in 16 possible outcomes.

https://mbtitraininginstitute.myersbriggs.org

Strong Interest Inventory

An interest inventory and career assessment tool.

https://www.cpp.com/products/strong/index.aspx

Knowledge is Power

Francis Bacon

GOALS

Educational goals enable career growth. Whether you've earned a college degree, certificate of completion, or acquired a work related certification, you have secured a brighter future for yourself. Better-trained people get better jobs.

What is the earning power of a college education? According to the 2010 U.S. Census Bureau, income generally correlates with a person's level of education.

Average annual income
High School $34,000.
Associates $45.000.
Bachelors $60,000.
Masters $70,000.
Doctorate $88,000.
Professional $104,000.

Education is often times a means to an end. It is preparation for the type of career field you are entering. With that in mind, it is important to know what employers are looking for from their employees.

ELEVEN KEY ATTRIBUTES EMPLOYERS EVALUATE
by Stephen A. Laser Associates

- Energy and impact
- Maturity and self-confidence
- Communication skills
- Interpersonal skills
- Planning and organizing
- Initiative and work attitude
- Responsiveness to guidance and direction
- Tolerance for stress and frustration
- Sales orientation and ability
- Customer-service orientation
- Leadership orientation and ability

PATHWAYS

There are several pathways to a college degree. There are many pathways to your educational goals.

Traditional Higher Education

Attending a "brick and mortar" school to receive lecture style: classroom instruction. You may be a resident student or off campus.

College Credit for High school Coursework and Exams
AP (Advanced Placement)

Credit by Exam

Get credit for what you already know. You can "proficiency out" of taking college courses through testing. (Schools set passing scores and determine what exams are accepted.)

Undergraduate Proficiency Exams
CLEP (College Level Education Program)
DSST (DANTES Subject Standardized Tests)
ECE (Excelsior College Exam)

Language Credentialing
TOEFL (Test of English as a Foreign Language)
DLPT (Defense Language Proficiency Test)

Practice Exams
Peterson's
AP, CLEP & TOEFL

Prior Learning Assessment
CAEL (Counsel for Adult and Experiential Learning)

There are no fewer than 263 colleges and universities who currently offer this option. Work (paid or volunteer), community activities, hobbies, travel, independent study, and some types of non-formal education may count toward college credit. Typically, a portfolio is used to document this life experience.

Distance Education

- Correspondence Courses
- Recorded Media
- Computer Based Instruction on CD ROM or Networked
- Courses via the Internet
- Satellite Conferencing

Live as if you were to die tomorrow. Learn
as if you were to live forever.
Gandhi

MILITARY

Apprenticeships

USMAP (United Services Military Apprenticeship Program)

Used by the Navy, Marine Corps and Coast Guard to document service members training and skills learned while performing their military jobs.

Participating Trades

- Aircraft Mechanic
- Automobile Mechanic
- Carpenter
- Computer Operator
- Cook
- Counselor
- Crash and Rescue
- Diesel Mechanic
- Electrician
- Electronics Mechanic
- Fire Fighter
- Machinists
- Maintenance Mechanic
- Nondestructive Tester
- Operating Engineer
- Police Officer
- Power Plant Operator
- Refrigeration Mechanic Welder

Military Experience

ACE (American Counsel on Education) evaluates and assigns college level credit recommendations for each of the following:

Military Schools & Training
Occupations
Pay Grades

The highest result of education is tolerance.
Helen Keller

EDUCATIONAL ACRONYMS

AARTS **Army/American council on education Registry Transcript System**

ASVAB **Armed Service Vocational Aptitude Battery**

ATT **Apprenticeship Technical Training**

CCAF **Community College of the Air Force**

DANTES **Defense Activity for Non-Traditional Education Support**

DLAB **Defense Language Aptitude Battery**

DLPT **Defense Language Proficiency Test**

DSST **DANTES Subject Standardized Tests**

MGIB **Montgomery General Issue Bill**

MTS **Master Training Specialist**

Navy COOL **Navy Credentialing Opportunities On-Line**

OAP **Officer Ascension Programs**

SOC **Servicemembers Opportunity Colleges**

TA **Tuition Assistance**

VMET **Verification of Military Education and Training**

VOLED **VOluntary Education Program**

MAJORS

COMMUNITY COLLEGES

- Accounting
- Art
- Auto Mechanic
- Aviation Technology
- Business Administration
- Computer Maintenance Technology
- Computer Science
- Cosmetology
- Criminal Justice
- Data Processing
- Dental Hygiene
- Engineering Technology
- Fire Science
- General Studies
- Interior Design
- Legal Assistant
- Liberal Arts
- Medical Assistant
- Nursing
- Real Estate
- Secretarial Science
- Technician
- Travel Management

LIBERAL ARTS COLLEGES
Basic Skills

- English Composition
- Math

Social Sciences

- Black Studies
- Cultural Anthropology
- Economics
- Government
- History
- Political Science
- Psychology
- Sociology
- Western Civilization

Natural Sciences

- Astronomy
- Biology
- Botany
- Chemistry
- Earth Science
- Geography
- Geology
- Meteorology
- Oceanography
- Physical Anthropology
- Physics
- Zoology

Humanities

- Art
- Drama
- Foreign Language
- Literature
- Music

- Philosophy
- Religion
- Speech

That's not all. There are 900 college majors available. Name it and it probably exists. Refer to <u>Book of Majors</u> by CollegeBound.

A liberal education frees a man from the prison-house of his class, race, time, place, background, family and even his nation.
Robert Hutchins

DR. ROBERT MCCLERREN

CURRICULUM BY DOMAIN

As used by Beloit College

Systems (*foundational systems*)

These courses, among other things, provide the foundations for communication and discourse, for scientific inquiry, and for reasoning itself. The focus of Systems courses is on these foundational concepts, as well as the many rules and principles that govern their systemic relationship and application. Within this domain, students develop an applied, working knowledge of the various relational principles that govern a foundational system (e.g. calculus, math, music theory, logic, modern and classical languages).

Arts (*creative practices*)

Courses in this domain engage students' mastery of techniques and sharpen their aptitude for creative abstraction and its use in the imaginative process. The goals of courses in this domain include instructing students on approaches and techniques used for creating conceptual material for an audience, introducing standards of creative practice, training students on observation and critique of their own and others' work, and cultivating technical proficiency necessary for the creative discipline (e.g. computer visualization, entrepreneurship, dance technique, visual arts, music technique, creative writing, theatre).

Behavior (*social analysis of human behavior*)

Students explore approaches and models that enhance our understanding of human behavior within a variety of cultural and social contexts, both contemporary and historical. These courses may also address the implications of social science research for public policy formation (e.g. history, anthropology, religious studies, economics, political science).

BE PREPARED

An investment in Knowledge always pays the best interest.
Benjamin Franklin

The Universe *(scientific inquiry into the physical and biological universe)*

In these courses, students formulate and test hypotheses about the physical and biological universe by gathering, analyzing, and interpreting empirical data in laboratory and/or field settings. Students develop abilities to evaluate scientific evidence and may also develop an understanding of the applications of science for local, national, and global issues (e.g. physical and biological sciences, biologically oriented anthropology and psychology).

Texts *(textual cultures and analysis)*

This domain concerns the study and critical analysis of texts. Courses in this domain examine the connections and coherence between the discourse and contexts from which it stems. Students learn how to engage texts, both as reader and respondent, and they develop the interpretative and analytic skills necessary for responsible engagement with texts (e.g. literature, philosophy, history, social sciences).

The direction in which education starts a
man will determine his future life.
Plato

UNDERGRADUATE ADMISSIONS

Admission policies vary among schools. Some schools set minimum test score requirements to standardized exams as part of their admission procedure. Depending on the school, and degree level, these exams may determine your eligibility to get started.

High School Equivalency
GED (General Education Development)
High School Completion Programs

Undergraduate Program Admissions
ACT (American College Testing)
ASSET
College Placement Exams
SAT (Scholastic Aptitude Testing)

Practice Exams
Peterson's
ACT, Praxis, SAT

BE PREPARED

TEACHER CERTIFICATION

PRAXIS

Praxis is a practical application or exercise of a branch of learning. Praxis Exams are required to earn a teaching certificate in most states.

I PPST (Pre-Professional Skills Test) Academic skills: reading writing & math.
II PLT (Principles of Learning & Teaching)
II MSAT (Multiple Subjects Assessment for teachers)
III Classroom Performance Assessments

Education's purpose is to replace an
empty mind with an open one.
Malcolm Forbes

GRADUATE ADMISSIONS

For the expert academic advisement for advanced degrees, refer to <u>Roadmap for Graduate Study</u> by Dr. Donald C. Martin. This is a one of a kind, comprehensive guide for prospective graduate students. Their checklist and application process leaves nothing to chance.

Graduate Program Admissions
GMAT (Graduate Management Admissions Test)
GRE (Graduate Record Exams)
LSAT (Law School Admissions Test)
MAT (Miller Analogies Test)
MCAT (Medical College Admission Test)

Practice Exams
Peterson's
GMAT, GRE, LSAT, MAT, MCAT

If you put off everything till you're sure of
it, you'll never get anything done.
Norman Vincent Peale

ACCREDITATION

ACCREDITED INSTITUTIONS OF POSTSECONDARY EDUCATION

Does going to an "accredited" school really matter? It does any time you need to transfer credits. More importantly, potential employers may not view your qualifications as valid if you received a degree from a non accredited school. Find out and know where you stand.
An accrediting body must be recognized by the U.S. Department of Education to authorize accrediting status to a school.

Regionally accredited schools
They are predominantly academically oriented, non-profit institutions. The majority of Colleges/Universities, both public and private, hold this type of accreditation. The U.S. is divided into 6 geographic regions. Schools seeking Regional Accreditation can only become accredited through the accrediting body serving their geographic region. Transferring credits from one regionally accredited school to another is common, regardless of which region the school belongs to.

Nationally accredited schools
They are predominantly for-profit and offer vocational, career or technical programs. Upstart schools and those specializing in distance learning; also tend to hold this type of accreditation. A Nationally accrediting body may award accreditation to any school, regardless of geographic location. Nationally accredited schools recognized credit transfers between schools of like accreditation.
Regionally accredited schools and Nationally accredited schools serve different purposes. The academic standards are

different and the process for accreditation is different. Students should NOT expect credits to transfer from a Nationally accredited school to a Regionally accredited school.

Apart from accreditation, each college has the right to set policy and accept or refuse credit transfers.

We are all faced with a series of great opportunities
brilliantly disguised as insoluble problems.
John W. Gardner

FINANCIAL AID

Federal Programs
FAFSA (Free Application for Federal Student Aid)
Pell Grants are valued from $555. to $5,550.

Military Grants and Scholarships
Financial Aid for Veterans, Military Personnel, and Their Dependents
by Reference Service Press

School Scholarships
Nearly every college awards scholarships unique to that school. Their financial aide department will have information on what scholarships are available, what the qualifications are, and how to apply.

Private Scholarships
Various Organizations and Associations offer scholarships for college.

Public Scholarships
Scholarships Grants & Prizes
by Peterson's

Veterans Grants
Some states fund grants for veterans in the amount of 120 semester hours at a state school.

Work Study
Schools have various forms of compensating students such as stipends as part of assistantships or internships, or working a service job on campus.

Section 2

NON-DEGREE OPTIONS

ALTERNATIVES TO A COLLEGE EDUCATON

INFORMAL LEARNING

Learning to gain knowledge (Not for credit).

Studying a subject no longer requires signing up for college classes. Learn at your convenience via professionally developed courseware. If you are seeking self-improvement, ready to explore new interests, or just enjoy a challenge; consider one of the options below. These resources work well for standardized test preparation.

CBI (Computer Based Instruction)

Below are general areas of study. For specific course listings, go to the Edmentum website, click on "Resources" and then "Course Catalog." Check "Show all descriptions" for course descriptions.

- American History
- Biology
- Business Basics Reading
- Chemistry
- Earth and Space Science
- Economics
- Geography
- Life Science
- Life Skills
- Math
- Physical Science
- Social Studies
- Technology Fundamentals
- U.S. Government
- Writing

Courses on DVD and Audio CD

The Great Courses offers courses taught by top College Professors. (Not for credit) They currently have a library of over 250 courses specifically developed for lifelong learners.

Categories

- Better Living
- Economics & Finance
- Fine Arts
- High School
- History
- Literature & Language
- Mathematics
- Music
- Philosophy & Intellectual History
- Professional
- Religion
- Science

The beautiful thing about learning is that no
one can take it away from you.
B. B. King

CREDENTIALS WITHOUT A COLLEGE DEGREE

There are alternatives to college degrees. Other forms of credentialing can be obtained in many fields of study. This is another way to document your qualifications, and set yourself apart from others in your vocation.

CERTIFICATES

Offered in lieu of college degrees or as an addition to a college degree. Certificates are available at each level of higher education (Undergraduate, Graduate and Post Graduate).

College Certificates (sampling)

- Accounting
- Administrative Assistant
- Assistant Tourism
- Basic Computer Applications Skills
- Business Management
- Community Planning
- Community Police Officer
- Computer Engineering
- Consumer Marketing
- Emergency Management
- General Studies
- Graduate Certificate in Business
- Graduate Certificate in Information Technology
- Graduate Certificate in Patient Safety
- Graphics Specialist
- Health Care Management
- Information Systems
- Instructional Design

- Legal Office
- Marketing
- Medical Office Assistant
- Medical Transcription
- Performance Consulting
- Post-Master's Certificate in Health Care
- Post-Master's Certificate in Nursing Administration
- Prior Learning Assessment
- Process Management
- Public Health Management
- School Nurse Certificate
- Supervision
- Tax Practitioner
- Training and Development
- Web Designer
- Word Processing

Education is an ornament in prosperity and a refuge in adversity.
Aristotle

CERTIFICATIONS

Issued by non-government agencies, associations and companies. The following 32 career fields have 778 certifications offered through 270 different associations. Navy Cool is a clearinghouse of certifications. https://www.cool.navy.mil/usn/index.htm You do not need to be military to access this information. Click on full credential search, and then enter your subject in search. As an example, "computer" will yield 15 related certifications and the institution granting them.

Career Field Certifications (sampling)

- Arts
- Aviation
- Business Management
- Communications
- Computers
- Construction and Building
- Dental
- Education Leadership
- Electronics
- Emergency
- Energy and Power
- Engineering
- Finance and Accounting
- Fire and Rescue
- Food
- Human Resources
- Information Technology
- Intelligence
- Law Enforcement and Security
- Legal
- Lodging
- Logistics

- Mechanical and Industrial
- Medical
- Music
- News and Media
- Office and Administrative Support
- Ordnance
- Photography
- Postal Services
- Purchasing and Supply
- Religion
- Restaurant
- Science
- Special Operations
- Telecommunications
- Transportation
- World Languages

Who Benefits From Occupational Certifications?

- Laborers & Tradesmen needing career oriented Certifications
- Employees advancing in the workforce
- Full time workers too busy to be a full time student
- Individuals with limited income

A wise man will make more opportunities than he finds.
Francis Bacon

Appendix A

FIVE PHILOSOPHIES OF EDUCATION

LIBERAL

PURPOSE(S)
   To develop intellectual powers of the mind; to enhance the broadest sense of learning; to provide a general, "well-rounded" education.

LEARNER(S)
   "Renaissance person"; always a learner; seeks knowledge; expected to gain a conceptual and theoretical understanding.

TEACHER ROLE
   The "expert"; transmitter of knowledge; teaches students to think; clearly directs learning process.

CONCEPTS/KEY WORDS
   Liberal arts; learning for its own sake; general and comprehensive education; critical thinking; traditional knowledge; academic excellence.

METHODS
   Lecture; reading and critical analysis; question-and-answer; teacher-led discussion; individual study; standardized testing.

PEOPLE & PRACTICES
   Aristotle, Plato, Adler, Rousseau, Piaget, Houle, Great Books Society, Paideia Program, Center for the Study of Liberal Education, Chautauqua, Elderhostel.

BEHAVIORAL

PURPOSE(S)
To promote competence, skill development and behavioral change; ensure compliance with standards and societal expectations.

LEARNER(S)
Learners not involved in setting objectives; master one step before another; practice behaviors/skills to get them right.

TEACHER ROLE
Manager, controller; authoritative; sets expectations; predicts and directs learning outcomes.

CONCEPTS/KEY WORDS
Standards-based; mastery learning; competence; behavioral objectives; performance; practice, feedback/reinforcement; accountability.

METHODS
Computer-based instruction, lock-step curriculum, skill training, demo & practice, criterion-referenced testing.

PEOPLE & PRACTICES
Thorndike, Watson, Skinner, Tyler, Mager, vocational training, management-by-objectives, certification exams, military training, religious indoctrination.

PROGRESSIVE

PURPOSE(S)
To support responsible participation in society; to give learners practical knowledge and problem-solving skills.

LEARNER(S)
Learner needs, interests, and experiences are valued and become part of learning process; learner takes an active role in learning.

TEACHER ROLE
Organizer; guides learning process; provides real-life learning applications; helps learners work cooperatively.

CONCEPTS/KEY WORDS
Problem-solving; practical learning; experience-based; needs assessment; transfer of learning: active inquiry; collaboration; social responsibility.

METHODS
Projects; scientific or experimental method; simulations; group investigation; cooperative learning; portfolios.

PEOPLE & PRACTICES
Dewey, Whitehead, Lindeman, community college developmental studies, citizenship education, cooperative extension, university without walls, community schools.

HUMANISTIC

PURPOSE(S)
To enhance personal growth and development; to facilitate individual self-actualization.

LEARNER(S)
Learner is highly motivated and self-directed; assumes responsibility for learning; very involved in planning learning projects.

TEACHER ROLE
Facilitator; helper; mutual participant in teaching-learning exchange; supports learning process.

CONCEPTS/KEY WORDS
Freedom; autonomy; individuality; teaching-learning exchange; self-directedness; interpersonal communication; openness; authenticity; feelings.

METHODS
Experiential learning; discovery learning; open discussion; individual projects; collaborative learning; independent study; self-assessment.

PEOPLE & PRACTICES
Rogers, Maslow, Knowles, Tough, group dynamics, self-directed learning, I'm OK, You're OK; diversity education, credit for prior learning.

RADICAL

PURPOSE(S)
To bring about, through education, fundamental social, cultural, political, and economic changes in society.

LEARNER(S)
Learner and "teacher" are equal in learning process; personal autonomy; learner is empowered; voluntary participant.

TEACHER ROLE
Coordinator; convener; equal partner with learner; suggests but does not determine directions.

CONCEPTS/KEY WORDS
Consciousness-raising; praxis; noncompulsory learning; autonomy; social action; empowerment-social justice; commitment; transformation.

METHODS
Critical discussion and reflection; problem-posing; analysis of media output; social action theater.

PEOPLE & PRACTICES
Holt, Freire, Illich, Kozol, Shor, Ohliger, Perelman, free school movement, Afro-centrism, voter registration/education, social justice education.

Appendix B

COLLEGES WITH THE GREAT BOOKS PROGRAM

Colleges with the Great Books Program

Azusa Pacific University Honors College	Azusa	CA
Baylor University, Great Texts	Waco	TX
Biola University, Torrey Honors Institute	La Mirada	CA
Boston University	Boston	MA
Columbia University	New York	NY
Dharma Realm Buddhist University	Ukiah	CA
East Carolina University Thomas Harriot College of Arts and Sciences	Greenville	NC
Faulkner University	Montgomery	AL
Fordham University, Rose Hill, Honors Program	New York	NY
Franciscan University of Steubenville	Steubenville	OH
George Fox University, William Penn Honors Program	Newberg	OR
Gutenberg College	Eugene	OR
Harrison Middleton University	Tempe	AZ
Hillsdale College	Hillsdale	MI
Houston Baptist University, Honors College	Houston	TX
Mercer University	Macon	GA
Middlebury College	Middlebury	VT
New York University, Gallatin Program, Liberal Studies Program	New York	NY
Palm Beach Atlantic University	West Palm Beach	FL
Pepperdine University	Malibu	CA
Saint Anselm College	Goffstown	NH
Saint Mary's College of California, Integral Liberal Arts Program	Moraga	CA
Shimer College	Chicago	IL
St. John's College	Annapolis	MD
Northeast Catholic College	Warner	NH
The Templeton Honors College at Eastern University	St. Davids	PA

Thomas Aquinas College	Santa Paula	CA
Thomas More College of Liberal Arts	Merrimack	NH
University of Chicago	Chicago	IL
University of Dallas	Irving	TX
University of San Francisco, St. Ignatius Institute	San Francisco	CA
University of Notre Dame	Notre Dame	IN
University of Michigan	Ann Arbor	MI
University of Texas at Austin, Thomas Jefferson Center	Austin	TX
University of West Florida, Kugelman Honors Program	Pensacola	FL
Wyoming Catholic College	Lander	WY

Learning is a treasure that will follow its owner everywhere.
Chinese Proverb

Appendix C

PRIOR LEARNING
ASSESSMENT COLLEGES

Prior Learning Assessment Colleges (by state)

Andrew Jackson University	Birmingham	AL
Faulkner University	Montgomery	AL
Judson College	Marion	AL
Spring Hill College	Mobile	AL
University of Alabama	Tuscaloosa	AL
University of Mobile	Mobile	AL
Alaska Pacific University	Anchorage	AK
Gateway Community College	Phoenix	AZ
Harrison Middleton University	Tempe	AZ
Ottawa University	Phoenix	AZ
Rio Salado College	Multiple locations	AZ
University of Phoenix	Phoenix	AZ
Western International University	Tempe	AZ
Biola University	La Mirada	CA
Chapman University	Orange	CA
Dominican Univeristy of California	San Rafael	CA
Fielding Graduate University	Santa Barbara	CA
Golden Gate University	Multiple locations	CA
Institute for Business Performance	San Jose	CA
Life Pacific College	San Dimas	CA
National University	La Jolla	CA
Saint Mary's College of California	Moraga	CA
Trident University International	Cypress	CA
University of Redlands	Redlands	CA
University of the Pacific	Stockton	CA
Art Institute of Colorado	Denver	CO
Colorado Christian University	Lakewood	CO
Colorado Technical University Online	Multiple locations	CO

Nazarene Bible College	Colorado Springs	CO
Regis University	Denver	CO
Albertus Magnus College	New Haven	CT
Charter Oak State College	New Britain	CT
Eastern Connecticut State University	Willimantic	CT
Gateway Community College	New Haven	CT
Norwalk Community College	Norwalk	CT
University of Connecticut	Storrs	CT
University of New Haven	West Haven	CT
Howard University	Washington	DC
Strayer University	Washington	DC
Potomac College	Washington	DC
Washington International University	Wilmington	DE
Barry University	Miami Shores	FL
Eckerd College	St. Petersburg	FL
Miami Dade College	Miami	FL
National-Louis University	Tampa	FL
Northwood University	West Palm Beach	FL
Palm Beach Atlantic University	West Palm Beach	FL
Saint Leo University	Saint Leo	FL
Southeastern University	Lakeland	FL
Stetson University	Deland	FL
Albany State University	Albany	GA
Georgia State University	Atlanta	GA
Black Hawk College	Moline	IL
College of DuPage	Glen Ellyn	IL
DePaul University	Chicago	IL
Eastern Illinois University	Charleston	IL
Elmhurst College	Elmhurst	IL
Governors State University	University Park	IL

Greenville College	Greenville	IL
Hebrew Theological College	Skokie	IL
Joliet Junior College	Joliet	IL
Lewis University	Romeoville	IL
Lincoln Christian University	Lincoln	IL
Lincoln College	Lincoln	IL
Millikin University	Decatur	IL
National-Louis University	Wheeling	IL
North Park University	Chicago	IL
Parkland College	Champaign	IL
Robert Morris University	Multiple locations	IL
Rock Valley College	Rockford	IL
The Chicago School of Professional Psychology	Chicago	IL
University of Chicago Medical Center	Chicago	IL
University of Illinois at Springfield	Springfield	IL
University of St. Francis	Joliet	IL
Calumet College of St. Joseph	Whiting	IN
Huntington University	Huntington	IN
Indiana Institute of Technology	Fort Wayne	IN
Indiana University Purdue University	Fort Wayne	IN
Indiana University Purdue University	Indianapolis	IN
Indiana University School of Continuing Studies	Gary	IN
Ivy Tech Community College of Indiana	Multiple locations	IN
Marian College	Indianapolis	IN
Martin University	Indianapolis	IN
Ottawa University	Jeffersonville	IN
Saint Mary-of-the-Woods College	Woods	IN
University of Indianapolis	Indianapolis	IN
Ashford University	Clinton	IA

Buena Vista University	Storm Lake	IA
St. Ambrose University	Davenport	IA
Upper Iowa University	Fayette	IA
Baker University	Multiple locations	KS
Fort Hays State University	Hays	KS
Friends University	Wichita	KS
Johnson County Community College	Overland Park	KS
Ottawa University	Ottawa	KS
Southwestern College	Winfield	KS
Tabor College	Hillsboro	KS
Ashland Community & Technical College	Ashland	KY
Bowling Green Tech College	Bowing Green	KY
Eastern Kentucky University	Richmond	KY
Gateway Community and Technical College	Florence	KY
Mid-Continent University	Mayfield	KY
Midway College	Midway	KY
Spalding University	Louisville ·	KY
University of Louisville	Louisville	KY
Bossier Parish Community College	Bossier City	LA
Delgado Community College	New Orleans	LA
Northwestern State College University	Natchitoches	LA
Kaplan University	South Portland	ME
Anne Arundel Community College	Arnold	MD
Montgomery College	Multiple locations	MD
Stevenson University	Owings Mills	MD
University of Maryland University College	Adelphi	MD
Washington Adventist University	Takoma Park	MD
Boston University	Boston	MA
Bunker Hill Community College	Boston	MA
Cambridge College	Multiple locations	MA

Lesley University	Cambridge	MA
North Shore Community College	Danvers	MA
Springfield College	Springfield	MA
Suffolk University	Boston	MA
Central Michigan University	Mount Pleasant	MI
Concordia University	Ann Arbor	MI
Cornerstone University	Grand Rapids	MI
Davenport University	Multiple locations	MI
Madonna University	Livonia	MI
Miller College	Battle Creek	MI
Northwood University	Midland	MI
Spring Arbor University	Spring Arbor	MI
Capella University	Minneapolis	MN
Century College	White Bear Lake	MN
Inver Hills Community College	Inver Grove Heights	MN
Metropolitan State University	Brooklyn Park	MN
North Hennepin Community College	Brooklyn Park	MN
St. Mary's University of Minnesota	Multiple locations	MN
Jackson State University	Jackson	MS
Evangel University	Springfield	MO
Grantham University	Kansas City	MO
Metropolitan Community Colleges	Multiple locations	MO
Missouri Southern State University	Joplin	MO
Webster University	Webster Groves	MO
William Woods University	Fulton	MO
Bellevue University	Bellevue	NE
Chadron State College	Chadron	NE

Midland Lutheran College	Fremont	NE
Nebraska Wesleyan University	Lincoln	NE
Franklin Pierce University	Rindge	NH
Granite State College	Concord	NH
New Hampshire Technical Institute	Concord	NH
Southern New Hampshire University	Manchester	NH
Berkeley College	Woodland Park	NJ
Bloomfield College	Bloomfield	NJ
Centenary University	Hackettstown	NJ
Thomas Edison State College	Trenton	NJ
Berkeley College	New York	NY
Bronx Community College	Bronx	NY
College of New Rochelle	New Rochelle	NY
Empire State College (SUNY)	Saratoga Springs	NY
Excelsior College	Albany	NY
Kaplan University	Manhattan	NY
Keuka College	New York	NY
Manhattan College	New York	NY
Marist College	Poughkeepsie	NY
Medaille College	Buffalo	NY
Medgar Evers College	New York	NY
Metropolitan College	New York	NY
New York University	New York	NY
Nyack College	New York	NY
Roberts Wesleyan College	Rochester	NY
St. Joseph's College	Multiple locations	NY
Suffolk County Community College	Multiple locations	NY
University College of Syracuse University	Syracuse	NY
Winston-Salem State University	Winston-Salem	NC

Bismarck State College	Bismark	ND
University of Mary	Bismark	ND
Antioch University	Yellow Springs	OH
Ashland University	Ashland	OH
Baldwin-Wallace College	Berea	OH
Bluffton University	Bluffton	OH
College of Mount St. Joseph	Cincinnati	OH
Columbus State Community College	Columbus	OH
Cuyahoga Community College	Cleveland	OH
Lourdes College	Sylvania	OH
Malone University	Canton	OH
Mount Vernon Nazarene University	Mount Vernon	OH
Northwest State Community College .	Archbold	OH
Ohio Christian University	Circleville	OH
Ohio Northern University	Ada	OH
Ohio University	Athens	OH
Sinclair Community College	Dayton	OH
The Union Institute & University	Cincinnati	OH
The University of Akron	Akron	OH
University of Northwestern Ohio	Lima	OH
Wilberforce University	Wilberforce	OH
Langston University	Multiple locations	OK
Mid-America Christian University	Oklahoma City	OK
Oklahoma City Community College	Oklahoma City	OK
Southern Nazarene University	Bethany	OK
University of Oklahoma	Norman	OK
Corban College	Salem	OR
George Fox University	Newberg	OR
Linfield College	McMinnville	OR
Marylhurst University	Marylhurst	OR
Southern Oregon University	Ashland	OR
Warner Pacific College	Portland	OR

Warner Pacific College	Portland	OR
Albright College	Reading	PA
Baptist Bible Seminary	Clarks Summit	PA
California University Of Pennsylvania	California	PA
Delaware County Community College	Multiple locations	PA
Delaware Valley College	Multiple locations	PA
Elizabethtown College	Elizabethtown	PA
Gwynedd-Mercy College	Multiple locations	PA
Holy Family University	Multiple locations	PA
Immaculata College	Immaculata	PA
Lancaster Bible College	Lancaster	PA
Millersville University of Pennsylvania	Millersville	PA
Misericordia University	Dallas	PA
Neumann University	Aston	PA
Peirce College	Philadelphia	PA
Pennsylvania College of Technology	Williamsport	PA
Pennsylvania State University	University Park	PA
Point Park University	Pittsburgh	PA
Rosemont College	Rosemont	PA
Wescoe School of Muhlenberg College	Allentown	PA
Widener University	Chester	PA
Wilkes University	Wilkes-Barre	PA
South Dakota State University	Brookings	SD
Austin Peay State University	Clarksville	TN
Bethel College, Success Program	Mckenzie	TN
Christian Brothers University	Memphis	TN
Lincoln Memorial University	Harrogate	TN
Roane State Community College	Harriman	TN
Tennessee State University	Nashville	TN

Trevecca Nazarene University	Nashville	TN
University of Tennessee at Martin	Martin	TN
Dallas Baptist University	Dallas	TX
Lamar University	Beaumont	TX
LeTourneau University	Longview	TX
Northwood University	Cedar Hill	TX
Our Lady of the Lake University	San Antonio	TX
Southwestern Assemblies of God University	Waxahachie	TX
St. Edward's University	Austin	TX
University of the Incarnate Word	Alamo Heights	TX
Wiley College	Marshall	TX
Utah Valley University	Orem	UT
Western Governors University	Salt Lake City	UT
Westminster College	Salt Lake City	UT
Community College of Vermont	Montpelier	VT
Johnson State College	Johnson	VT
Regent University	Virginia Beach	VA
City University of Seatle	Seatle	WA
Northwest University	Kirkland	WA
Spokane Falls Community College	Spokane	WA
American Public University System	Charles Town	WV
Mountain State University	Beckley	WV
Alverno College	Milwaukee	WI
Cardinal Stritch University	Milwaukee	WI
Concordia University	Mequon	WI
Edgewood College	Madison	WI
Marian College of Fond Du Lac	Fond Du Lac	WI
Mount Mary College	Milwaukee	WI
National-Louis University	Milwaukee	WI
Ottawa University	Brookfield	WI
University of Wisconsin Extension	Lancaster	WI
Viterbo University	La Crosse	WI

Appendix D

GLOSSARY OF
EDUCATIONAL TERMS

Glossary of Educational Terms

Academic Probation

A student may be placed on Academic Probation if their GPA falls below 2.0. In that event the student would be given the following semester to bring the GPA above 2.0 and continue their studies. Not achieving a 2.0 GPA or higher would terminate their studies.

Accreditation

Is the record that an educational institution maintains an established level of academic standards.

ACE (American Council on Education)

ACE is the major coordinating body for nearly 1,800 colleges and universities. Institutions that are ACE members more easily transfer credits between one another, and recognize credit recommendations for military training.

ACT (American College Testing)

The ACT® test is the nation's most popular college entrance exam accepted and valued by all universities and colleges in the United States. The ACT is based on what students learn in high school and provides personalized information about their strengths for education and career planning.

Add

The time period in the beginning of each term, when a course may be added to a student's schedule.

Adler, Mortimer J.

Mortimer Jerome Adler (December 28, 1902 – June 28, 2001) was an American philosopher, educator, and popular author. He worked for Columbia University, the University of

Chicago, Encyclopedia Britannica, and Adler's own Institute for Philosophical Research. His seminal work was "The Great Ideas, A Lexicon of Western Thought," published in 1952.

Admissions
The process of entering a college or any other institution of post-secondary education. Accepted for admission means you will be allowed to register for and attend classes.

Adult Education
Adult education is post secondary education apart from schooling that typically occurs immediately following High School graduation.

AP (Advanced Placement)
A program in the United States and Canada created by the College Board, which offers college-level curricula and examinations to high school students.

Applied Science Degrees
An Associate of Applied Science (A.A.S) is a technical degree. It is also referred to as a terminal degree because once completed, no higher degree will be pursued. Courses taken for an A.A.S. degree (e.g. English composition) may not meet the same academic requirements at those for an A.S. or B.S. degree.

Articulation Agreements
Are agreements between a high school and postsecondary institutions. Content of courses between institutions is compared to allow like coursework in High Schools to count as college coursework completed. This guards against duplicating coursework in college that students have already completed in High School.

Arts vs. Science Degrees

The primary difference between the two types of degrees is the focus of the coursework students are required to complete in order to earn them. Generally, coursework for "Science" degrees are more concentrated in the major field of study, while "Arts" degrees give more latitude in choosing electives.

ASSET Test

The ASSET® program is a series of short placement tests developed by ACT. It helps you identify your strengths as well as the knowledge and skills you will need in order to succeed in specific subject areas. ASSET also helps your school use this information to guide you toward classes that strengthen and build logically upon your current knowledge and skills.

Associates Degree

An associate degree is an undergraduate academic degree awarded by colleges and universities upon completion of a course of study lasting two years. The first associate degrees were awarded the U.S. in 1898.

Audit

Auditing a course allows a student to take a class without the benefit of a grade or credit for a course. It is an opportunity for self-enrichment and way to explore other academic areas without affecting the students GPA.

Bachelors Degree

A bachelor's degree is an undergraduate academic degree awarded by colleges and universities upon completion of a course of study lasting four years.

CAEL (Counsel for Adult and Experiential Learning)

Advocates the use of "Prior Leaning Assessment" toward

educational and career goals. Individual's learning from work and life experience, can be applied to educational goals: earning their degrees and credentials faster and expediting their career goals.

Capstone

A capstone course, also known as capstone unit serves as the culminating and usually integrative experience of an educational program.

CBI (Computer based instruction)

The use of the computer in the delivery of instruction. Other similar terms include: CBT (Computer Based Training), CAI (Computer Assisted Instruction) and CAL (Computer Assisted Learning).

CBT (Computer based training)

Any course of instruction whose primary means of delivery is a computer. A CBT course (sometimes called courseware) may be delivered via a software product installed on a single computer, through a corporate or educational intranet, or over the Internet as Web-based training.

Certificates

Many college certificate programs prepare students to obtain the professional credentials they need to gain employment or advance in their careers. Some college certificates are awarded as a student progresses in an undergraduate or graduate-level degree program. Regardless of their application, certificates of completion require a set number of courses (four or more) in a particular field of study.

Certifications

Professional certifications are sought where a person must

show competency in performing a job or task, usually by the passing of an examination. Some colleges offer training in preparation for certification testing. Some professional certifications also require that one apprentice in a related field. Some professional certifications are valid for a lifetime upon completing all certification requirements. Others expire after a certain period of time and have to be maintained with further education and/or testing.

CLEP (College Level Examination Program)
A group of standardized tests created and administered by College Board. These tests assess college-level knowledge in thirty-six subject areas and provide a mechanism for earning college credits without taking college courses. They are administered at more than 1,700 sites (colleges, universities, and military installations) across the United States. There are about 2,900 colleges, which grant CLEP credit. Each institution awards credit to students who meet the college's minimum qualifying score for that exam, which is typically 50 to 60 out of a possible 80, but varies by site and exam. These tests are useful for individuals who have obtained knowledge outside the classroom, such as through independent study, homeschooling, job experience, or cultural interaction; and for students schooled outside the United States. They provide an opportunity to demonstrate proficiency in specific subject areas and bypass undergraduate coursework. Many take CLEP exams because of their convenience and lower cost (typically $80) compared to a semester of coursework for comparable credit.

Clock Hours
One semester credit hour is equal to at least 37.5 clock hours of instruction.

Cohort

The cohort program came into being, based on the idea of community in education. It is a group of students band together, taking the same classes at the same time for the full term of the degreed program.

College

College is a degree awarding educational institution or a constituent within a university.

Colloquium

A colloquium is a course where the instructor assigns readings for each session which are then discussed by the members.

Common App (Common Application)

It is an undergraduate college admission application used to apply to any of 693 member colleges and universities. Common Application Incorporated, a not-for-profit association, manages the process. Its mission is to promote access, equity, and integrity in the college admission process, which includes subjective factors gleaned from essays and recommendations alongside more objective criteria such as class rank and standardized testing.

Common Core

The Common Core State Standards Initiative is an educational initiative in the United States that details what K–12 students should know in English language arts and mathematics at the end of each grade. The initiative is sponsored by the NGA (National Governors Association) and the CCSSO (Council of Chief State School Officers) and seeks to establish consistent educational standards across the states as well as ensure that students graduating from high school are prepared to enter credit-bearing courses at two or four-year college programs or to enter the workforce.

Community College

A community college is a type of educational institution geared toward conferring Associates degrees along with continuing education and vocational training.

Continuing Education

Includes degree credit courses by non-traditional students, non-degree career training, workforce training, formal personal enrichment courses (both on-campus and online) self-directed learning (such as through Internet interest groups, clubs or personal research activities) and experiential learning as applied to problem solving.

Core Knowledge Sequence

A foundation that conducts research on curricula; develops books and other materials for students, parents, and teachers; and serves as a training and communications hub for schools using Core Knowledge. The Foundation has developed a number of publications, including general information packets about Core Knowledge, the Sequences, textbooks, and other supplementary materials for use in conjunction with the Sequence. The Core Knowledge Foundation also offers a variety of staff development workshops to facilitate the process of implementing the Core Knowledge program in schools and hosts an annual national conference, which focuses on the sharing of ideas between educators at every level and making connections across the Core Knowledge network.

Correspondence Courses

In 1883 the first official recognition of correspondence education took place at Chautauqua College of Liberal Arts,

New York. The college granted degrees to students who successfully completed academic work through correspondence education and summer workshops. These courses grew to become the International Correspondence School. In 1915, following a call by academicians to research the effectiveness of correspondence education vs. traditional education, the NUEA (National University Extension Association) was formed. The NUEA set out to establish new national level guidelines for credit transferal, for acceptance of credit from correspondence courses, and for quality standards for correspondence educators.

Credentials

A credential is an attestation of qualification, competence, or authority issued to an individual by a third party with a relevant or de facto authority or assumed competence to do so. Examples of credentials include academic diplomas, academic degrees, certifications, security clearances, identification documents, badges, passwords, user names, keys, and powers of attorney.

Credit by Exam

The most accepted among Colleges and Universities are CLEP, DANTES and ECE exams. Credit Recommendations. The ACE (American Council on Education) College Credit Recommendation Service was established in 1974 to connect workplace learning with colleges and universities by helping students gain access to academic credit for formal training taken outside traditional degree programs. With over 35,000 programs reviewed, ACE is the national leader in the evaluation process for education and training obtained outside the classroom including courses, exams, apprenticeships, and other types of nontraditional forms of training.

Curriculum Vitae

A curriculum vitae is a written overview of a person's experience and other qualifications for a job opportunity. In some countries, a CV is typically the first item that a potential employer encounters regarding the job seeker and is typically used to screen applicants, often followed by an interview. CVs may also be requested for applicants to postsecondary programs, scholarships, grants and bursaries. Applicants can provide electronic text of their CV to employers using email, an online employment website or using a job-oriented social networking service' website, such as LinkedIn.

Developmental Courses

Generally courses that have course numbers starting with a zero or numbers less than 100 are considered developmental courses, or courses that prepare students for college-level courses. While these courses will not count toward your degree requirements, they are great "refresher" courses to help improve your math and writing skills (and increase the likelihood of success) when you do take regular college courses.

Discussion

A collaborative exchange of ideas between a facilitator and students for the purpose of intellectual inquiry.

Dissertation

A research paper written as a requirement for the Doctor of Philosophy degree.

Distance Education

Distance education or Distance Learning is the education of students who may not always be physically present at a brick and mortar school. Traditionally, this involved taking courses wherein the student corresponded with the school via mail. Today it involves online education. Courses of study that are hybrid, blended or 100% technology can be considered Distance Education.

Doctorate Degree

An academic degree awarded by universities that is, in most countries, a research degree that qualifies the holder to teach at the university level in the degree's field, or to work in a specific profession. There are a variety of doctoral degrees, with the most common being the Doctor of Philosophy (PhD), which is awarded in many different fields, ranging from the humanities to the scientific disciplines. There are also some doctorates in the US, such as the Juris Doctor (JD), Doctor of Medicine (MD) and Doctor of Osteopathic Medicine (DO), which are generally regarded internationally as professional degrees rather than doctorates, as they are not research degrees and no defense of any dissertation or thesis is performed. Many universities also award honorary doctorates to individuals who have been deemed worthy of special recognition, either for scholarly work or for other contributions to the university or to society.

Drop

The period of time at the beginning of a term, where a student is allowed to cancel taking a class without penalty.

ECE (Excelsior College Examinations)

A series of tests offered by Excelsior College in New York. Many colleges and universities will grant college credits for each test, although they are not as widely accepted as CLEP and DSST. ECE's can be transferred to more than 2,500 accredited colleges across the U.S. The exam administration period is 3 hours and the tests currently cost between $235 and $335. Most ECE exams are considered equivalent to 3 semester hours of college credit.

EdD (Doctor of Education)

A doctoral degree that has a research focus in the field of education. It prepares the holder for academic, research, administrative, clinical or professional positions in educational, civil, private organizations or public institutions.

Electives

An elective course is one chosen by a student from a number of optional subjects or courses in a curriculum, in addition to required courses.

Endorsements

For K-12 teacher candidates and secondary teacher candidates, the primary endorsement is in the individual's major. For elementary education teachers, the endorsement is in their specialization.

Enrollment

Enrollment occurs when the student has accepted the offer of being admitted by the school.

ESL (English as a Second Language)

A course of study designed for individuals with different native languages. These same students may also be categorized as EFL (English as a foreign language).

Expiration of Credits

Undergraduate college credits don't ever expire, however graduate college credits generally have a lifespan of 5 years

FAFSA (Free Application for Federal Student Aid)

A form that can be prepared annually by current and prospective college students (undergraduate and graduate)

in the United States to determine their eligibility for student financial aid.

Fees

A student fee is a fee charged to students at a school, college, university or other place of learning that is in addition to any matriculation and/or tuition fees. It may be charged to support student organizations and student activities (for which it can be called an activity fee) or for intercollegiate programs such as intramural sports or visiting academics; or, at a public university or college, as a means to remedy shortfalls in state funding (in which case it can often be called a technology fee). Further fees may then be charged for features and facilities such as insurance, health and parking provision.

Financial Aide

Student financial aid in the United States is funding that is available exclusively to students attending a post-secondary educational institution in the United States. This funding is to assist in covering the many costs incurred in the pursuit of post-secondary education. Financial aid is available from federal, state, educational institutions, and private agencies foundations, and can be awarded in the forms of grants, education loans, work-study and scholarships.

Foreign Transcript Evaluation

Performed by independent agencies for the purpose of transferring college credits earned outside the United States.

GED (General Education Development)

ACE, in Washington DC, owns the GED trademark. These tests measure proficiency in science, mathematics, social studies, reading, and writing. Passing the GED test gives those who do not complete high school, or who do not meet requirements for high school diploma, the opportunity to earn their high school equivalency credential, also called a high school equivalency diploma or general equivalency diploma.

General Education Requirements

English, History, Science and Mathematics. The core academic subjects you studied in high school are also the subjects make up the bulk of general education courses in college. No matter what major you pursue, you'll have to take one or two classes in each of the major academic disciplines. Depending on the focus of the university you attend, you may also need to take courses in religion, culture or a foreign language.

GMAT (Graduate Management Admission Test)

A CAT (computer adaptive test) intended to assess certain analytical, writing, quantitative, verbal, and reading skills in written English for use in admission to a graduate management program, such as an MBA. It requires knowledge of certain grammar and knowledge of certain algebra, geometry, and arithmetic. The GMAT does not measure business knowledge or skill, nor does it measure intelligence. According to the test owning company, the GMAT assesses analytical writing and problem-solving abilities, while also addressing data sufficiency, logic, and critical reasoning skills that it believes to be vital to real-world business and management success. It can be taken up to five times a year. Each attempt must be at least 16 days apart.

Graduate Assistant

Graduate teaching assistants (often referred to as GTAs or simply TAs) are graduate students employed on a temporary contract by a department at a college or university in teaching-related responsibilities.

Graduate Studies

Permission to begin Graduate studies is granted by a graduate school to students who have successfully completed a bachelor's degree with GPA of 3.0 or higher.

Grant

A grant is a sum of money given for a specific purpose. Governmental agencies and benevolent organizations often earmark funds for educational advancement.

GRE (The Graduate Record Examination)

Is a standardized test that is an admissions requirement for most Graduate Schools in the United States. The GRE is owned and administered by ETS (Educational Testing Service) who created it in 1949. According to ETS, the GRE aims to measure verbal reasoning, quantitative reasoning, analytical writing, and critical thinking skills that have been acquired over a long period of learning. The content of the GRE consists of certain specific algebra, geometry, arithmetic, and vocabulary.

Great Books of the Western World

A 54-volume set of books originally published in the United States in 1952, by Encyclopedia Britannica, Inc. The original editors had three criteria for including a book in the series: the book must be relevant to contemporary matters, and not only important in its historical context; it must be rewarding to re-read; and it must be a part of "the great conversation about the great ideas."

Great Ideas

Mortimer Adler compiled a list of great ideas that have collectively defined Western thought for more than 2,500 years. He began writing in alphabetical order beginning with ""Angel"" and ending with ""World."" The essays, originally published in the Syntopicon, were and remain the centerpiece of Encyclopedia Britannica's Great Books of the Western World. These essays, never before available except as part of the Great Books, are, according to Clifton Fadiman, Adler's finest work. Each essay—""'War and Peace,'"" ""'Love,'"" ""'God,'"" ""'Truth'""—treats each idea as if the original authors—from Homer to Freud, from Marcus Aurelius to Virginia Woolf— whose writings the ideas are drawn from, were sitting around a table, deep in conversation. His purely descriptive synthesis presents the key points of view on almost 3,000 questions without endorsing or favoring any one of them. More than a thousand pages, containing more than half a million words on more than two millennia of Western thought, The Great Ideas is a fitting capstone to the career of Mortimer J. Adler.

Harvard Classics

A 61-volume anthology of classic works of literature, compiled in 1909, by Harvard president Charles W. Eliot. This set of books is also known as the 6-foot shelf.

High School Diploma Programs

Passing the GED is to certify academic skills at the high school level, but sets the bar much lower than an actual high school education. Adults with a high school diploma or GED earn an average of $11,000 per year more than adults who haven't finished high school (US Census Bureau). Furthermore, those with diplomas make considerably more than those with GEDs. Penn Foster is one such institution that offers a High School Diploma program.

Highly Qualified

The highly qualified teacher provision is one of the goals of the No Child Left Behind Act (NCLB) of 2001. The term highly qualified teachers (HQT) comes from the original language of Title II (Preparing, Training, and Recruiting High Quality Teachers and Principals) of the No Child Left Behind Act. Title II of NCLB designates federal funds to educational agencies for the purpose of improving the student achievement through the professional development of highly qualified teachers and principals.

Hirsch, E.D.

An American educator and academic literary critic. He is professor emeritus of education and humanities at the University of Virginia. He is best known for writing Cultural Literacy: What Every American Needs to Know (1987), and is the founder and chairman of the Core Knowledge Foundation.

Humanities

Humanities are academic disciplines that study aspects of human culture. In the Middle Ages, the term contrasted with divinity and referred to what is now called classics, the main area of secular study in universities at the time. Today, the humanities are distinguished from studies that include the physical and social sciences. The humanities generally in include language, literature, philosophy, religion, art and music.

Hutchins, Robert

January 17, 1899 – May 17, 1977, was an American educational philosopher, dean of Yale Law School (1927–1929), and president (1929–1945) and chancellor (1945–1951) of the University of Chicago. While he was president of the University of Chicago, Hutchins implemented wide-ranging and controversial reforms of the University, including the elimination of varsity football. The most far-reaching reforms involved the undergraduate College of the University of Chicago, which was retooled into a novel pedagogical system built on Great Books, Socratic dialogue, comprehensive examinations and early entrance to college. Although the substance of this Hutchins Plan was abandoned by the University shortly after Hutchins resigned in 1951, an adapted version of the program survives at Shimer College in Chicago.

ID (Independent Study)
A form of education offered by many high schools, colleges, and other educational institutions. It is sometimes referred to as directed study, and is an educational activity undertaken by an individual with little to no supervision. Typically a student and professor or teacher agree upon a topic for the student to research with guidance from the instructor for an agreed upon amount of credits. Independent studies provide a way for well-motivated students to pursue a topic of interest that does not necessarily fit into a traditional academic curriculum. They are a way for students to learn specialized material or gain research experience. Also, independent studies provide students opportunities to explore their interests deeper and make important decisions about how and where they will direct their talents in the future.

ILE (Integrated Learning Environment)
An ILE is a collection of learning-centric enterprise class applications that are tied together to simplify and extend the benefits of electronic learning.

Internship
An internship is job training for white collar and professional careers. Internships for professional careers are similar in some ways but not as rigorous as apprenticeships for professions, trade and vocational jobs. They lack the standardization and oversight of their counterpart. Interns may be college or university students, high school students, or post-graduate adults. These positions may be paid or unpaid and are usually temporary.

Intersession

Is a short break or mini-term between the traditional, standard academic terms. An intersession may be a period of a few weeks between semesters or quarters during which students can take short, accelerated classes or complete other academic work.

LSAT (Law School Admissions Test)

The LSAT is a half-day standardized test administered four times each year at designated testing centers throughout the world. It is administered by the LSAC (Law School Admission Council) for prospective law school candidates, the LSAT is designed to assess reading comprehension, logical, and verbal reasoning proficiencies. The test is an integral part of the law school admission process in the United States, Canada (common law programs only), the University of Melbourne, Australia, and a growing number of other countries. An applicant cannot take the LSAT more than three times within a two-year period. The test has existed in some form since 1948, when it was created to give law schools a standardized way to assess applicants aside from GPA.

Lecture Instruction

A lecture is an oral presentation intended to present information or teach people about a particular subject, for example by teacher. Lectures are used to convey critical information, history, background, theories, and equations. A politician's speech, a minister's sermon, or even a businessman's sales presentation may be similar in form to a lecture. Usually the lecturer will stand at the front of the room and recite information relevant to the lecture's content.

Liberal Arts Education

The liberal arts are those subjects or skills that classically are considered essential for a person to know in order to take an active part in civic life (public debate, defending oneself in court, serving on juries, and military service). Grammar, logic, and rhetoric were the core liberal arts, and to a lesser degree: arithmetic, geometry, the theory of music, and astronomy. Liberal arts education can refer to academic subjects such as literature, philosophy, mathematics, and social and physical sciences, or it can also refer to overall studies in a liberal arts degree program.

Lifelong Learner

Lifelong learning is inclusive of both formal and informal learning opportunities throughout people's lives. It fosters the continuous development and improvement of the knowledge and skills needed for employment and personal fulfillment.

Life Skills

Life skills are abilities for adaptive and positive behavior that enable people to deal effectively with the demands and challenges of everyday life. They are a set of skills acquired via teaching or direct experience that are used to handle problems and questions commonly encountered in daily life. The subject varies greatly depending on social norms and community expectations but skills that functions for well-being and aid individuals to develop into active and productive members of their communities are considered as life skills.

Lower Level

Freshman and Sophomore level courses.

Masters Degree

A master's degree is awarded by universities or colleges upon demonstrating mastery of a specific field of study or area of professional practice. A master's degree normally requires previous study at the bachelor's level, either as a separate degree or as part of an integrated course. Master's graduates are expected to possess advanced knowledge of a specialized body of theoretical and applied topics; high order skills in analysis, critical evaluation, or professional application; and the ability to solve complex problems and think rigorously and independently.

MAT (Miller Analogies Test)

A standardized test used primarily for graduate school admissions in the United States. Created and still published by Harcourt Assessment (now a division of Pearson Education). The MAT consists of 120 questions in 60 minutes. It is a verbal based test offered via computer.

Matriculation

Matriculation is the formal process of entering a university, or of becoming eligible to enter by fulfilling certain academic requirements such as a matriculation examination.

MCAT (Medical College Admission)

The MCAT is a computer-based standardized examination for prospective medical students in the United States, Australia, Canada, and Caribbean Islands. It is designed to assess problem solving, critical thinking, written analysis and knowledge of scientific concepts and principles. The exam has been computer-based since January 27, 2007.

Multiple Intelligences

The theory developed by Howard Gardner in 1983 concerning learning styles. The 7 original categories are: Musical-rhythmic and harmonic, Visual-spatial, Verbal-linguistic, Logical-mathematical, Bodily-kinesthetic, Interpersonal, and Intrapersonal. He later added Naturalistic and Existential.

NADLP (Nationally Accredited Distance Learning Program) A publication by DANTES.

Non Formal

Non-formal learning is a loosely defined term covering various structured learning situations, such as swimming sessions for toddlers, community-based sports programs and conference style seminars, which do not either have the level of curriculum, syllabus, accreditation and certification associated with "formal learning."

Non Traditional

Non-traditional education includes students that part-time in status and whose age are older than the "traditional" student entering college immediately after graduating High School.

Official Transcript

In education, a transcript is an inventory of the courses taken and grades earned of a student throughout a course of study. Official transcripts are those sent directly from the school issuing it, to another school or potential employer. Transcripts issued to the student are not considered official.

Orientation

Student orientation is a period of time at the beginning of the academic year at a university during which a variety of events are held to orient and welcome new students.

PhD (Doctor of Philosophy)

Is a type of doctoral degree awarded by universities in many countries. Ph.D.'s are awarded for a wide range of programs in the sciences. The completion of a Ph.D. is often a requirement for employment as a university professor, researcher, or scientist in many fields. A clear distinction is made between an "earned doctorate", which is awarded for completion of a course of study and a thesis or dissertation.

PLA (Prior Learning Assessment)
PLA, describes a process used by regulatory bodies, adult learning centres, career development practitioners, military organizations, human resource professionals, employers, training institutions, colleges and universities around the world to evaluate skills and knowledge acquired outside the classroom for the purpose of recognizing competence against a given set of standards, competencies, or learning outcomes.

Placement Exams
Offered by colleges to determine the need for developmental courses.

Placement Services
Placement Services often include vacancy bulletin subscriptions, mailing of placement credentials, access to professional career counselors, job fairs and Graduate School Days, Career Library materials and assessment tools, workshops, and our extensive employer contact information. Minimal service fees are charged for these services.

Portfolio
Portfolios are used as a method of documenting life experiences to prove knowledge skills and abilities in a specific subject.

Post Graduate Studies
Postgraduate education studies are academic or professional degrees, academic or professional certificates, academic or professional diplomas conferred "post" masters. It is generally referred to as a doctoral program.

Practice Exams

Peterson's test preparation products include live and online courses, live and online practice tests, as well as printed study guides. They cover a wide range of topics including: SAT, ACT, PSAT, AP Exams, CLEP, TOEFL, ASVAB, EMT, postal service, case worker, law enforcement, and more. They also offer several free and paid practice tests on their website.

Practicums

A practicum is often a requirement in a specialized field of study, such as nursing. This gives students supervised practical application of a previously or concurrently studied theory. Practicums are a student teaching requirement, and a part of credentialing students with social work majors.

Praxis

A Praxis test is one of a series or American teacher certification exams of American exams written and administered by the Educational Testing Service. Various Praxis tests are usually required before, during, and after teacher training courses in the U.S.

Private Schools

Local, state or national governments do, not administer private schools. The schools themselves reserve the right to select their students. They are funded in whole or in part by charging their students tuition, and do not receive public tax dollars.

Professional Studies

"Professional studies" is a term used to classify academic programs, which are applied or interdisciplinary in focus. The term can also be used for non-academic training for a specific profession. Students are trained to ensure expected standards and adequate service delivery in the best practice of a profession.

Proficiency
Proficiency exams are administered to individuals who wish to prove they have sufficient knowledge in a subject, equivalent to a student who has taken a college class. If the predetermined score is achieved, the student is award course credits.

Programmed Learning
Programmed learning uses preordered or "programed" sequence of instruction. Each subject matter is presented with a corresponding tested sequence. After each step, learners are given a question to test their comprehension. Then immediately the correct answer is shown. This means the learner at all stages makes responses, and is given immediate feedback of results.

Progress Check
After reading the lessons, Self-Progress Checks (tests) are offered at the end of each module. A passing score must be achieved, before the learner is allowed to proceed. Once all the Module progress checks have been accomplished, the learner is prepared to take the Final Examination for that particular subject.

Proprietary
Schools that own intellectual property, have propriety wrights over its distribution and use.

Provisional Student
Provisional students are applicants who do have a high school diploma or its equivalent but do NOT have the credentials required for regular degree admission (such as adequate high school grade-point average, SAT scores, and/or adequate Carnegie units).

Public Schools

Public Schools are generally state schools that offer primary and secondary and postsecondary education. They are public because they are funded by both local and state tax dollars.

Publishing

A stipulation made by colleges or universities for professors, as a contingency for tenure; especially by schools considered "research" institutions.

Quarter

In the United States, quarters typically comprise 10 weeks of class instruction. Academic quarters first came into existence as such when William Rainey Harper organized the University of Chicago on behalf of John D. Rockefeller in 1891.

Quarter Hours

A quarter hour of instruction equals 25 clock hours.

Reciprocal Agreements

Transferring a teaching certificate from one state to the next is generally not an academic problem. Most states will charge fee to handle and process the paperwork, review the teacher's existing credentials, and produce a new license for use in that state's classroom.

Recommendations

A recommendation is a document in which the writer assesses the qualities, characteristics, and capabilities of the person being recommended. It should cite individual's ability to perform a particular task or function. Letters of recommendation are typically related to employment. Others may be in regard to admission to institutions of higher education, or scholarship eligibility. Recommendation letters are usually specifically addressed to a particular requester.

References
A reference page is a list of your references, which you will need to supply to your potential employer. Typically, employers ask for three references, but that number can vary.

RCE (Regents College Examinations)
In New York State, Regents Examinations are statewide-standardized examinations in core high school subjects required for a Regents Diploma to graduate. Regents diplomas are optional and typically offered for college-bound and non-disabled students. Most students, with some limited exceptions, are required to take the Regents Examinations. To graduate, students are required to have earned appropriate credits in a number of specific subjects by passing yearlong or half-year courses, after which they must pass Regents examinations in some of the subject areas. For higher achieving students, a Regents with Advanced designation, and an Honor designation, are also offered.

Regionally Accredited
Regional accreditation is the educational accreditation of schools, colleges, and universities in the United States by one of seven regional accrediting agencies. Accreditation is a voluntary process by which colleges demonstrate to each other, and sometimes to employers and licensing agencies, that their credits and degrees meet minimum standards. It is the self-regulation of the higher education industry.

Registration
Registration is the process of establishing your identity with an institution.

Research
The systematic investigation into and study of materials and sources in order to establish facts and reach new conclusions.

Residency Requirements
For degree-seeking students, a credit hour residency requirement indicates the number of credits you must complete with that school for them to confer a degree. It does not mean that you must physically come to the University or attend courses at any physical location.

Resume
A document used by a person to present their backgrounds and skills. Résumés can be used for a variety of reasons, but most often they are used to secure new employment. A typical résumé contains a "summary" of relevant job experience and education. The résumé is usually one of the first items, along with a cover letter and sometimes an application for employment, which a potential employer sees regarding the job seeker and is typically used to screen applicants, often followed by an interview.

SAT (Scholastic Aptitude Testing)
The SAT is a standardized test widely used for college admissions in the United States. Introduced in 1926, its name and scoring have changed several times; originally called the Scholastic Aptitude Test, it was later called the Scholastic Assessment Test, then the SAT I: Reasoning Test, then the SAT Reasoning Test, and now, simply the SAT.

Scholar
A specialist in a particular branch of study, especially the humanities; a distinguished academic.

Scholarship   a grant or payment made to support a student's education, awarded on the basis of academic or other achievement.

Scientific Method
Discovery through experimentation, measurement and testing.

Semester
Each semester runs a time span of 16 weeks.

Semester Hours
One semester (trimester) credit hour is equal to at least 37.5 clock hours of instruction.

Seminar
A seminar is a form of academic instruction. It is comprised of small groups that hold recurring meetings; each time focusing on some particular subject, in which everyone present is requested to actively participate. It is based on the Socratic method of teaching as guided instruction. Discussions related to assigned readings are initiated through a facilitator.

SME (Subject Matter Expert) or domain expert is a person who is an authority in a particular area or topic.

Split Term
Schools on the semester system may also offer split term courses, which run for 8 weeks only.

Standardized Tests
A standardized test is a test that is administered and scored in a consistent, or "standard", manner. Standardized tests are designed in such a way that the questions, conditions for administering,

scoring procedures, and interpretations are consistent and are administered and scored in a predetermined, standard manner.

Stipend

A stipend is a form of salary, such as for an internship or an apprenticeship. It is often distinct from an income or a salary.

Student Loan

A student loan is a type of loan designed to help students pay for post-secondary education and the associated fees, such as tuition, books and supplies, and living expenses. It may differ from other types of loans in that the interest rate may be substantially lower and the repayment schedule may be deferred while the student is still in school.

Syllabus

A syllabus document that defines the course, outlines its objectives and identifies the expectations and responsibilities of the student.

Teacher Certification

Is the credentialing document issued by each sate authorizing teachers to teach in pre-school, primary or secondary schools.

Tenure

A tenured appointment is an indefinite appointment that can be terminated only for cause or under extraordinary circumstances such as financial exigency or program discontinuation.

Thesis

A thesis is a document submitted in support of candidature for an academic degree or professional qualification presenting the author's research and findings. The word "thesis" is most often used in cognate with completing a masters degree.

TOEFL (Test of English as a Foreign Language)

A standardized test to measure the English language ability of non-native speakers wishing to enroll in English-speaking universities. Many English-speaking academic and professional institutions accept the test. TOEFL is one of the two major English-language tests in the world, the other being the IELTS.

Trade School

A vocational school (trade school or vocational college) is a type of educational institution designed to provide vocational education, or technical skills required to perform the tasks of a particular and specific job. These schools prepare individuals to enter the workforce without the mandate of a college degree.

Traditional

Traditional education refers to long-established customs that society traditionally used in schools. Traditional teacher-centered methods focus on rote learning and memorization. The traditional approach is also concerned with objective educational standards based on testing.

Transcript Evaluation

A transcript evaluation is a process by which a receiving institution evaluates the courses a student has taken at another institution and counts them, where applicable, towards the student's degree plan.

Transferring

Almost all regionally accredited institutions only accept transfer credits from other regionally accredited institutions. This means that most state colleges and universities only accept credits from each other. However, students transferring from nationally accredited colleges may have to start their degrees over. Area specific regional accrediting bodies include the Southern Association of Colleges and Schools, the Middle States Commission on Higher Education and the New England Association of Schools and Colleges. National organizations with regional accreditation include the Higher Learning Commission (HLC) and the Accrediting Commission for Community and Junior Colleges.

Tutorial
A tutorial course is where one or a small number of students work on a topic and meet with the instructor weekly for discussion and guidance.

U.S. Department of Education
The United States Department of Education is a Cabinet-level department of the United States government, which was created in 1980.

Undergraduate Studies
Undergraduate education is the post-secondary education. It includes all the academic programs up to the level of a bachelor's degree. For example, a college student working on a four-year degree is known as an undergraduate.

University
A university is an institution of higher learning, which grants academic degree in various disciplines. Universities typically provide undergraduate education and postgraduate education.

Upper Level   Junior and Senior level courses.

Vested
Vesting is to give an immediately secured right of present or future deployment. One has a vested right to an asset that cannot be taken away by any third party, even though one may

not yet possess the asset. As an example, money paid into a pension plan may be vested after five years.

Vocational

Vocational education is education that prepares people to work in a trade, a craft, as a technician, or in professional vocations such as engineering, accountancy, nursing, medicine, architecture, or law. Craft vocations are usually based on manual or practical activities and are traditionally non-academic but related to a specific trade or occupation. Vocational education is sometimes referred to as career education or technical education.

Withdraw

Period of time after the term begins, that a student can cancel a class without penalty.

Appendix E

VOCABULARY

There is no shortage of books, providing definitions of words, intended to increase your vocabulary. They contain pages of information about words, their derivation and meaning. Such exercises are tedious and time consuming. These are examples of usage. Many of the words we already know, we have learned by association. That's why working with synonyms is key to quickly building vocabulary. The problem with syllabuses is they tend to define one $10. word with another. That means looking up one word you are interested in, leads to another word you are also unfamiliar with.

Words capitalized in bold, are ones that have been known to appear on SAT exams. Each word is identified with its part of speech, and four words you are likely familiar with. Listing them in this manner allows you to quickly reference and review new words. You do not need to spend time going through long lessons just to learn a single word. If you need to know more about a particular word, that is time to make use of a Dictionary of Etymology. In the meantime, using the synonym method to learn words will build your vocabulary quickly.

ABATE	v	decrease	lapse	lesson	subside
ABHOR	v	detest	disgust	hate	loath
ABJECT	a	contemptible	debased	degraded	wretched
ABRIDGE	v	compress	condense	reduce	shorten
ABSTEMIOUS	a	abstinent	moderate	sparing	temperate
ABSTRACT	a	conceptual	intangible	philosophical	theoretical
ABSTRUSE	a	mysterious	obscure	puzzling	scholarly
ABSURD	a	ludicrous	preposterous	ridiculous	unreasonable
ABUNDANCE	n	bounty	plenty	prosperity	wealth
ABUNDANT	a	ample	bountiful	copious	extravagant
ACCLAIM	n	admiration	fame	recognition	tribute
ACCLAIM	v	approve	commend	declare	welcome
ACCOMPLICE	n	ally	associate	assistant	partner
ACCORD	n	agreement	harmony	pact	understanding
ACCORDANCE	n	agreement	conformity	correspondence	harmony
ACCOST	v	address	greet	hail	salute

ACQUIESCE	v	agree	comply	consent	submit
ACQUISITION	n	acquirement	attainment	gain	purchase
ACQUISITIVE	a	covetous	desirous	greedy	selfish
ACRID	a	bitter	caustic	pungent	sharp
ACUTE	a	intense	perceptive	sharp	shrewd
ADAGE	n	motto	proverb	truism	saying
ADAMANT	a	immovable	insistent	unshakable	unyielding
ADEPT	a	able	clever	handy	skillful
ADJACENT	a	abutting	adjoining	bordering	proximate
ADJUNCT	n	accessory	addition	appendage	auxiliary
ADMONISH	v	advise	counsel	criticize	warn
ADMONITION	n	advice	caution	counsel	warning
ADORN	v	beautify	decorate	embellish	garnish
ADROIT	a	adept	clever	ingenious	skillful
ADVERSARY	n	competitor	enemy	opponent	rival
ADVERSE	a	dangerous	harmful	injurious	unfavorable
ADVOCATE	n	backer	defender	patron	supporter
AESTHETIC	a	appealing	artistic	beautiful	tasteful
AFFABLE	a	friendly	gentle	kind	pleasant
AFFINITY	n	attraction	connection	fondness	kinship
AFFLUENT	a	abundant	prosperous	rich	wealthy
AFFRONT	n	indignity	offense	slight	slur
AGENDA	n	schedule	plan	program	timetable
ALACRITY	n	eager	lively	prompt	swiftness
ALCHEMICAL	a	alchemic	chemical	pseudoscience	synthetic
ALIENATE	v	distance	divide	estrange	isolate
ALLEGED	a	assumed	pretended	so-called	supposed
ALLEGORY	n	fable	legend	myth	symbolic
ALLEVIATE	v	ease	lesson	reduce	relieve
ALLOT	v	allocate	apportion	assign	distribute
ALLUDE	v	hint	imply	refer	suggest
ALLURE	n	appeal	attractiveness	charm	enchantment
ALLURING	a	attractive	charming	enticing	fascinating
ALLUSION	n	hint	mention	reference	suggestion
ALOOF	a	arrogant	removed	standoffish	withdrawn
ALTERCATION	n	argument	disagreement	dispute	quarrel
ALTRUISTIC	a	charitable	compassionate	kind	selfless
AMALGAM	n	alloy	blend	combination	mixture
AMASS	v	accumulate	assemble	collect	gather
AMBIGUOUS	a	confusing	doubtful	uncertain	unclear
AMBITIOUS	a	difficult	eager	serious	weighty
AMBIVALENT	a	conflicted	doubtful	indecisive	uncertain
AMBULATORY	a	locomotive	mobile	moving	walking

AMELIORATE	v	amend	correct	improve	reform
AMENABLE	a	agreeable	compliant	obedient	submissive
AMIABLE	a	affable	amicable	cordial	friendly
AMITY	n	companionship	friendship	harmony	understanding
AMORPHOUS	a	formless	indefinite	shapeless	vague
ANALYSIS	n	examination	inquiry	investigation	study
ANARCHY	n	chaos	disorder	lawlessness	mayhem
ANECDOTE	n	fable	fiction	story	tale
ANIMATED	a	energetic	excited	lively	spirited
ANIMATION	n	energy	liveliness	spirit	vitality
ANIMOSITY	n	dislike	hatred	hostility	malice
ANNOTATED	v	commented	explained	interpreted	notated
ANONYMOUS	a	nameless	obscure	unidentified	unknown
ANTAGONISM	n	friction	hostility	opposition	rivalry
ANTAGONISTIC	a	contrary	hostile	opposed	unfriendly
ANTEDILUVIAN	a	ancient	antiquated	obsolete	old
ANTHOLOGY	n	album	collection	compilation	miscellany
ANTIDOTE	n	antitoxin	countermeasure	cure	remedy
ANTIQUATED	a	ancient	antique	obsolete	outdated
ANTITHETICAL	a	contrary	counter	opposing	opposite
APATHETIC	a	casual	indifferent	uninterested	unconcerned
APATHY	n	dispassion	emotionlessness	indifference	unconcern
APOCRYPHAL	a	counterfeit	fraudulent	illegitimate	unauthorized
APPALLING	a	awful	dreadful	hideous	shocking
APPEASE	v	assuage	disarm	pacify	soothe
APPREHEND	v	arrest	catch	perceive	understand
APPREHENSION	n	anxiety	dread	fear	worry
APPREHENSIVE	a	anxious	nervous	uneasy	worried
APPRISE	v	advise	inform	notify	tell
APT	a	fitting	proper	relevant	suitable
ARABLE	a	cultivatable	farmable	fertile	tillable
ARBITRARY	a	illogical	random	tyrannical	unreasoned
ARCANE	a	ambiguous	cryptic	mysterious	obscure
ARCHAIC	a	ancient	antiquated	obsolete	old-fashioned
ARCHIVE	n	chronicle	depository	record	register
ARDENT	a	enthusiastic	fervent	passionate	zealous
ARDUOUS	a	difficult	hard	laborious	strenuous
ARISTOCRACY	n	elite	gentry	nobility	upper-class
ARRAY	n	arrangement	assemblage	group	set
ARROGANCE	n	haughtiness	loftiness	pompousness	snootiness
ARROGANT	a	boastful	conceited	haughty	proud
ARTICULATE	a	eloquent	effective	fluent	well-spoken
ARTICULATE	v	enunciate	pronounce	voice	utter

ARTIFACT	n	antique	image	relic	ruin
ARTISAN	n	craftsman	handworker	journeyman	tradesman
ASCERTAIN	v	deduce	discern	discover	learn
ASCETIC	a	abstinent	austere	celibate	self-denying
ASPIRATION	n	ambition	desire	goal	hope
ASPIRING	a	ambitious	aspirant	enterprising	wishful
ASSAILANT	n	aggressor	attacker	assaulter	enemy
ASSENT	v	accept	agree	consent	sanction
ASSERT	v	affirm	declare	maintain	state
ASSESS	v	appraise	estimate	evaluate	judge
ASSET	n	advantage	benefit	boon	help
ASSIDUOUS	a	busy	diligent	hardworking	persistent
ASSUAGE	v	appease	pacify	relieve	satisfy
ASTUTE	a	clever	discerning	perceptive	shrewd
ATROPHY	v	decay	degenerate	deteriorate	wither
ATTEST	v	affirm	authenticate	certify	testify
ATTIRE	n	apparel	clothing	garment	outfit
ATTRIBUTE	n	characteristic	feature	trait	quality
ATTRIBUTE	v	accredit	ascribe	assign	impute
AUDIBLE	a	detectable	discernible	hearable	perceptible
AUGMENT	v	enlarge	expand	increase	supplement
AUSPICIOUS	a	encouraging	favorable	fortunate	promising
AUSTERE	a	harsh	serious	severe	stern
AUTHENTICATE	v	certify	confirm	validate	verify
AUTHENTICITY	n	actuality	conviction	fact	truth
AUTHORITARIAN	a	bossy	dictatorial	domineering	overbearing
AUTHORITATIVE	a	important	official	powerful	valid
AUTONOMY	n	free will	sovereignty	self-governance	volition
AVARICIOUS	a	covetous	greedy	mercenary	miserly
AVID	a	desirous	eager	enthusiastic	passionate
BANAL	a	clichéd	commonplace	conventional	ordinary
BANTER	n	jesting	repartee	witticism	wordplay
BARBARITY	n	brutality	cruelty	inhumanity	savagery
BASTION	n	castle	citadel	fort	stronghold
BEGUILING	a	alluring	bewitching	captivating	enticing
BELITTLE	v	bad-mouth	dismiss	disparage	trivialize
BELLIGERENT	a	aggressive	antagonistic	hostile	threatening
BENEFACTOR	n	backer	patron	sponsor	supporter
BENEFICENT	a	charitable	compassionate	humane	kindhearted
BENEFICIAL	a	advantageous	good	helpful	profitable
BENEFICIARY	n	heir	inheritor	recipient	successor
BENEVOLENCE	n	charity	generosity	goodwill	kindness
BENIGHTED	a	ignorant	illiterate	uneducated	unenlightened

BENIGN	a	favorable	harmless	healthful	kindly
BEQUEATH	v	entrust	grant	transfer	will
BEQUEST	n	endowment	gift	grant	legacy
BESTIAL	a	brutal	cruel	inhuman	savage
BIAS	n	favoritism	inclination	leaning	tendency
BIASED	a	one-sided	opinionated	partial	unfair
BIBLIOPHILE	n	booklover	bookworm	editor	reader
BIZARRE	a	eccentric	odd	peculiar	strange
BLASPHEMY	n	defilement	irreverence	profanity	sacrilege
BLITHE	a	blissful	cheerful	happy	joyful
BLUEPRINT	n	diagram	design	layout	plan
BOISTEROUS	a	noisy	riotous	uproarious	wild
BOLSTER	v	brace	prop	reinforce	support
BOMBASTIC	a	inflated	overblown	pompous	pretentious
BONDAGE	n	captivity	enslavement	serfdom	servitude
BOOR	n	bumpkin	clodhopper	peasant	yokel
BOURGEOISIE	n	middle class	populace	proletariat	public
BRAWN	n	might	muscle	power	strength
BRAWNY	a	burly	muscular	powerful	strong
BREADTH	n	amplitude	extent	scope	width
BREVITY	n	briefness	conciseness	shortness	succinctness
BURGEONING	a	budding	flowering	flourishing	growing
CACOPHONY	n	discord	disharmony	dissonance	harshness
CALLOUS	a	compassionless	cruel	insensitive	heartless
CANDID	a	direct	frank	honest	outspoken
CANTANKEROUS	a	argumentative	contentious	disagreeable	malicious
CAPACIOUS	a	broad	comprehensive	roomy	spacious
CAPITULATE	v	concede	relent	surrender	yield
CAPRICIOUS	a	fickle	changeable	flighty	impulsive
CAPTIVATE	v	charm	bewitch	enchant	fascinate
CASTIGATE	v	criticize	punish	rebuke	reprimand
CATASTROPHIC	a	damning	destructive	disastrous	ruinous
CATEGORICAL	a	absolute	certain	explicit	unqualified
CAUSTIC	a	acidic	corrosive	sarcastic	scathing
CELERITY	n	quickness	rapidity	speed	swiftness
CENSOR	v	blame	condemn	denounce	reprimand
CENSURE	v	condemn	criticize	denounce	scold
CHAGRINED	a	annoyed	offended	unhappy	upset
CHAOS	n	confusion	disorder	mayhem	turmoil
CHAOTIC	a	confused	disorderly	disorganized	wild
CHARADE	n	disguise	mockery	parody	pretense
CHARLATAN	n	fraud	hoaxer	impostor	sham
CHASTEN	v	chastise	discipline	correct	punish

CHIMERICAL	a	fictitious	imaginary	make-believe	mythical
CHRONICLER	n	annalist	biographer	historian	recorder
CIRCUMLOCUTION	n	long-windedness	redundancy	verbiage	wordiness
CIRCUMSPECT	a	careful	cautious	discreet	wary
CIRCUMVENT	v	avoid	bypass	evade	dodge
CITE	v	mention	name	quote	refer
CLAMOR	n	commotion	noise	racket	uproar
CLANDESTINE	a	concealed	covert	private	secret
CLARIFY	v	demonstrate	explain	illustrate	simplify
COALESCE	v	combine	connect	merge	unite
COERCE	v	force	compel	make	oblige
COHERENCE	n	cohesiveness	connection	continuity	integrity
COHERENT	a	logical	rational	reasonable	sound
COINCIDE	v	accord	agree	concur	correspond
COINCIDENTAL	a	accidental	casual	coinciding	concurrent
COLLABORATION	n	concert	cooperation	partnership	teamwork
COLLABORATIVE	a	collective	cooperative	joint	mutual
COLLECTIVE	a	common	communal	joint	united
COLLOQUIUM	n	conference	meeting	seminar	symposium
COLLUSION	n	complicity	connivance	conspiracy	plot
COLOSSAL	a	astronomical	gigantic	huge	immense
COMBATANT	n	champion	defender	fighter	warrior
COMBUSTIBLE	a	burnable	explosive	fiery	flammable
COMMENDABLE	a	admirable	good	laudable	praiseworthy
COMMODIOUS	a	ample	convenient	roomy	spacious
COMMONPLACE	a	average	everyday	ordinary	usual
COMMUNAL	a	community	popular	public	shared
COMPASSION	n	charity	kindness	pity	sympathy
COMPEL	v	coerce	force	oblige	require
COMPELLING	a	credible	convincing	irresistible	persuasive
COMPENSATE	v	offset	reimburse	repay	reward
COMPETENCE	n	ability	capability	expertise	skillfulness
COMPILE	v	accumulate	collect	compose	gather
COMPLACENT	a	apathetic	self-satisfied	smug	uninterested
COMPLEX	a	difficult	elaborate	intricate	involved
COMPLIANT	a	accommodating	cooperative	obedient	submissive
COMPLY	v	agree	conform	obey	yield
COMPOSURE	n	calmness	collectedness	self-control	serenity
COMPREHENSIBLE	a	clear	intelligible	plain	understandable
COMPREHENSIVE	a	all-inclusive	complete	exhaustive	thorough
CONCEDE	v	allow	admit	grant	yield
CONCILIATORY	a	disarming	pacifying	peacemaking	reconciling
CONCISE	a	brief	compact	summary	thumbnail

CONCLUSIVE	a	compelling	convincing	decisive	persuasive
CONCOCT	v	cook up	create	devise	invent
CONCOMITANT	a	accompanying	attendant	coincident	concurrent
CONCORDANCE	n	accord	agreement	consensus	harmony
CONCUR	v	accept	agree	coincide	coexist
CONDEMN	v	blame	criticize	rebuke	reprimand
CONDESCEND	v	descend	patronize	stoop	submit
CONDESCENSION	n	haughtiness	patronage	pride	smugness
CONDONE	v	accept	excuse	forgive	overlook
CONFIDANT	n	buddy	companion	comrade	friend
CONFIRM	v	affirm	certify	corroborate	substantiate
CONFLAGRATION	n	blaze	firestorm	inferno	wildfire
CONFORMITY	n	accordance	adherence	compliance	obedience
CONGENIAL	a	agreeable	friendly	pleasant	suitable
CONGREGATE	v	assemble	collect	gather	meet
CONJECTURE	n	guesswork	hypothesis	speculation	theory
CONNOISSEUR	n	authority	expert	guru	specialist
CONSCIENTIOUS	a	careful	honorable	thorough	upright
CONSEQUENCE	n	conclusion	effect	outcome	result
CONSPICUOUS	a	clear	noticeable	obvious	visible
CONSPIRACY	n	design	intrigue	scheme	plot
CONSPIRATORIAL	a	covert	hidden	secretive	sneaky
CONSTRAINT	n	coercion	duress	pressure	restraint
CONTEMPLATIVE	a	meditative	pensive	reflective	thoughtful
CONTEMPORARY	a	current	modern	new	present-day
CONTEMPORARY	n	companion	counterpart	equivalent	peer
CONTEMPT	n	hatred	disgust	disrespect	scorn
CONTEMPTUOUS	a	defiant	haughty	insulting	scornful
CONTENTION	n	argument	conflict	disagreement	strife
CONTEXT	n	background	circumstance	setting	situation
CONTINUITY	n	coherence	cohesion	flow	integrity
CONTRADICTION	n	denial	inconsistency	negation	rebuttal
CONTRITE	a	ashamed	apologetic	regretful	sorry
CONVENTIONAL	a	customary	normal	standard	traditional
CONVEY	v	carry	communicate	transfer	transmit
CONVICTION	n	assuredness	belief	confidence	reliance
CONVIVIAL	a	festive	jovial	merry	sociable
CONVOLUTED	a	complex	complicated	intricate	twisted
COPIOUS	a	abundant	ample	bountiful	plentiful
CORDIAL	a	cheerful	friendly	kindly	sociable
CORRELATE	v	associate	compare	connect	relate
CORRELATION	n	association	connection	relation	similarity
CORROBORATE	v	authenticate	certify	confirm	verify

CORRUPT	a	depraved	evil	immoral	wicked
CORRUPT	v	contaminate	defile	pollute	taint
CORRUPTION	n	depravity	immorality	perversion	vice
COUNTER	v	oppose	resist	return	reverse
COVERT	a	concealed	hidden	secluded	secret
COVETED	v	craved	desired	wanted	yearned
COVETOUS	a	desirous	grasping	greedy	moneygrubbing
CREDENCE	n	belief	confidence	faith	trust
CREDIBLE	a	believable	plausible	reliable	trustworthy
CREDULOUS	a	gullible	naive	impressionable	unsuspecting
CRITERION	n	benchmark	measure	specification	standard
CRITIQUE	n	analysis	commentary	criticism	review
CRUCIAL	a	critical	key	pivotal	vital
CRYPTIC	a	dark	deep	mysterious	obscure
CULPABLE	a	accountable	answerable	blameworthy	guilty
CUPIDITY	n	covetousness	desirous	greed	materialism
CURSORY	a	hasty	hurried	quick	rapid
CYNICAL	a	distrustful	pessimistic	skeptical	suspicious
CYNICISM	n	disbelief	distrust	doubt	suspicion
DEARTH	n	deficiency	lack	scarcity	shortage
DEBASE	v	corrupt	defile	degrade	devalue
DEBILITATE	v	exhaust	fatigue	tire	weaken
DEBUNK	v	discredit	expose	refute	uncover
DECADENT	a	degenerate	depraved	immoral	perverted
DECEIVE	v	bamboozle	fool	hoodwink	trick
DECEPTION	n	fraud	hoax	ruse	trickery
DECIPHER	v	decode	explain	interpret	solve
DECISIVE	a	conclusive	critical	crucial	final
DECORUM	n	manners	etiquette	politeness	propriety
DEDUCE	v	conclude	derive	gather	infer
DEDUCTION	n	discount	rebate	reduction	inference
DEFENDANT	n	accused	appellant	litigant	suspect
DEFERENCE	n	homage	respect	reverence	veneration
DEFIANT	a	bold	disobedient	insubordinate	rebellious
DEFLATE	v	chasten	discourage	humble	squash
DEFT	a	clever	dexterous	expert	skillful
DELIBERATE	v	consider	contemplate	debate	ponder
DELUGE	n	flood	inundate	overflow	torrent
DEMEANOR	n	attitude	bearing	behavior	conduct
DENIGRATE	v	bad-mouth	belittle	criticize	defame
DENOUNCE	v	blame	condemn	criticize	discredit
DEPICT	v	describe	portray	represent	show
DEPLETE	v	consume	empty	exhaust	spend

DEPLORABLE	a	disgraceful	dishonorable	inexcusable	shameful
DEPRAVED	a	corrupt	evil	immoral	wicked
DEPRAVITY	n	corruption	immorality	perversion	sinfulness
DERIDE	v	jeer	mock	ridicule	scoff
DERISION	n	mockery	ridicule	sarcasm	scorn
DERIVATIVE	a	imitative	offshoot	outgrowth	secondary
DESECRATE	v	defile	degrade	dishonor	violate
DESPICABLE	a	contemptible	mean	vile	wretched
DESULTORY	a	aimless	arbitrary	haphazard	random
DETER	v	discourage	inhibit	prevent	stop
DETERIORATE	v	decay	decline	degenerate	worsen
DETRIMENTAL	a	damaging	dangerous	harmful	hurtful
DEVIANT	a	aberrant	abnormal	irregular	unusual
DEVIL'S ADVOCATE	n	arguer	debater		
DEVIOUS	a	deceitful	dishonest	underhanded	unethical
DEXTEROUS	a	agile	handy	nimble	skillful
DIAGNOSIS	n	analysis	conclusion	examination	interpretation
DIALECT	n	idiom	language	speech	vernacular
DICTION	n	enunciation	phrasing	style	wording
DIDACTIC	a	edifying	educational	instructive	perceptive
DIFFERENTIATE	v	discern	discriminate	distinguish	separate
DIFFIDENT	a	bashful	meek	shy	timid
DIFFUSE	a	broadcast	distribute	scatter	spread
DIFFUSE	v	disperse	disseminate	distribute	spread
DIGRESS	v	deviate	ramble	stray	wander
DIGRESSION	n	departure	deviation	divergence	diversion
DILAPIDATED	a	decayed	ramshackle	shabby	tumbledown
DILEMMA	n	difficulty	plight	problem	trouble
DILIGENCE	n	attention	industry	perseverance	persistence
DILIGENT	a	careful	conscientious	hard-working	industrious
DIN	n	hubbub	racket	tumult	uproar
DIRE	a	appalling	awful	dreadful	grievous
DIRECTIVE	n	decree	edict	mandate	order
DISAFFECTED	a	disloyal	estranged	malcontent	unfriendly
DISCERN	v	distinguish	perceive	recognize	see
DISCERNING	a	discriminating	insightful	observant	perceptive
DISCERNMENT	n	insight	perception	wisdom	understanding
DISCLOSE	v	divulge	expose	reveal	show
DISCONCERTING	a	disturbing	confusing	unsettling	upsetting
DISCORD	n	conflict	disharmony	friction	strife
DISCORDANT	a	dissonant	harsh	inconsistent	inharmonious
DISCOURSE	n	dialogue	sermon	speech	talk
DISCOURSE	v	converse	lecture	orate	speak

DISCREET	a	careful	judicious	prudent	wise
DISCREPANCY	n	difference	disagreement	disparity	dissimilarity
DISCRETION	n	caution	choice	discernment	prudence
DISCRIMINATE	v	differentiate	discern	distinguish	separate
DISCRIMINATORY	a	differential	discerning	partial	selective
DISDAIN	n	contempt	despisement	despitefulness	dislike
DISGRUNTLED	a	displeased	dissatisfied	resentful	unhappy
DISMANTLE	v	breakdown	demolish	detach	disassemble
DISORIENT	v	befuddle	bewilder	confuse	perplex
DISOWN	v	deny	disclaim	reject	renounce
DISPARAGE	v	belittle	discredit	ridicule	scorn
DISPASSIONATE	a	fair	impartial	objective	neutral
DISPEL	v	banish	disperse	dissipate	scatter
DISPENSE	v	allocate	apportion	distribute	supply
DISPERSE	v	broadcast	distribute	scatter	spread
DISPOSITION	n	attitude	character	mindset	temperament
DISSECTION	n	analysis	examination	breakdown	deconstruction
DISSEMINATE	v	broadcast	circulate	distribute	spread
DISSENT	v	differ	disagree	clash	collide
DISSERTATION	n	discourse	essay	thesis	treatise
DISSONANT	a	inharmonious	off-key	unmelodious	unmusical
DISSUADE	v	discourage	inhibit	prevent	repel
DISTINCTIVE	a	characteristic	individual	peculiar	unique
DISTORT	v	falsify	misrepresent	twist	warp
DIVERGENT	a	conflicting	different	dissimilar	unalike
DIVERSE	a	assorted	different	distinct	various
DIVERSION	n	amusement	distraction	entertainment	recreation
DIVERSITY	n	assortment	miscellany	mixture	variety
DIVERT	v	alter	change	deflect	redirect
DIVULGE	v	disclose	expose	reveal	tell
DOCTORATE	n	degree	doctoral	doctorship	doctor's degree
DOCTRINE	n	belief	dogma	philosophy	principle
DOCUMENTATION	n	certification	corroboration	evidence	proof
DOGGED	a	determined	persistent	stubborn	tenacious
DOGMATIC	a	emphatic	insistent	opinionated	uncompromising
DOMAIN	n	area	realm	region	territory
DOMINATE	v	command	control	govern	rule
DOTAGE	n	decrepitude	feebleness	fuddy-duddy	senility
DOTARD	a	faltering	floundering	tottering	senile
DOUR	a	grim	glum	morose	sullen
DRASTIC	a	excessive	extreme	radical	severe
DROLL	a	amusing	humorous	ludicrous	odd
DRONE	v	chill	dillydally	loaf	lounge

DUBIOUS	a	doubtful	distrustful	questionable	suspicious
DUPE	n	chump	patsy	pushover	sucker
DUPE	v	con	deceive	defraud	trick
DUPLICITY	n	deceit	dishonesty	treachery	trickery
DWINDLE	v	decrease	decline	diminish	fade
EBULLIENT	a	cheerful	joyful	excitement	enthusiasm
ECCENTRIC	a	abnormal	irregular	outlandish	unconventional
ECLECTIC	a	assorted	diverse	extensive	varied
ECLIPSE	v	obscure	overshadow	outshine	surpass
ECSTATIC	a	blissful	happy	joyful	overjoyed
EDIFICATION	n	education	enlightenment	instruction	learning
EDIFICE	n	building	construction	erection	structure
EDIFYING	a	educational	enlightening	informal	instructive
EFFACE	v	eliminate	erase	remove	obliterate
EFFICACY	n	capability	efficiency	effectiveness	validity
EGALITARIAN	a	equal	classless	democratic	even-handed
EGOTIST	n	boaster	braggart	cynic	narcissist
EGREGIOUS	a	awful	dreadful	shocking	terrible
ELABORATE	a	complex	detailed	involved	sophisticated
ELATED	a	delighted	happy	joyful	jubilant
ELICIT	v	coax	extract	inspire	prompt
ELITE	a	aristocratic	champion	exclusive	supreme
ELITE	n	a-list	elect	nobility	upper class
ELITISM	n	advantage	exclusiveness	lordliness	snobbery
ELOQUENT	a	articulate	expressive	fluent	well-spoken
ELUCIDATE	v	clarify	explain	illuminate	illustrate
ELUDE	v	avoid	dodge	escape	evade
ELUSIVE	a	evasive	fugitive	shifty	slippery
EMACIATED	a	gaunt	haggard	starved	underfed
EMBED	v	enroot	entrench	implant	ingrain
EMBELLISH	v	adorn	decorate	enhance	exaggerate
EMIT	v	discharge	eject	exude	radiate
EMPATHY	n	accord	compassion	sympathy	understanding
EMPHATIC	a	assertive	forceful	insistent	positive
EMULATE	v	copy	follow	imitate	follow
ENAMORED	a	bewitched	charmed	infatuated	smitten
ENDEAVOR	n	attempt	effort	try	venture
ENDEAVOR	v	aim	seek	strive	undertake
ENDORSE	v	approve	ratify	sanction	support
ENERVATED	a	debilitated	exhausted	tired	weak
ENGAGING	a	attractive	captivating	charming	enchanting
ENGENDER	v	cause	create	generate	produce
ENGROSS	v	absorb	captivate	engage	occupy

ENHANCE	v	better	improve	increase	upgrade
ENIGMA	n	mystery	puzzle	secret	riddle
ENIGMATIC	a	baffling	mysterious	perplexing	puzzling
ENLIGHTEN	v	edify	inform	instruct	teach
ENLIGHTENMENT	n	edification	education	instruction	Nirvana
ENMITY	n	animosity	antagonism	hostility	malice
ENSCONCED	a	established	fixed	located	placed
ENSUE	v	arise	follow	pursue	succeed
ENTAIL	v	imply	involve	necessitate	require
ENTHRALL	v	captivate	enslave	mesmerize	thrill
ENTITY	n	being	essence	existence	individual
ENUMERATE	v	count	itemize	list	number
EPHEMERAL	a	fleeting	passing	short-lived	temporary
EPIC	a	heroic	gargantuan	grand	tremendous
EPIC	n	legend	narrative	saga	tale
EPITOME	n	ideal	model	representative	summary
EQUANIMITY	n	calmness	composure	poise	serenity
EQUIVOCATE	v	dodge	evade	hedge	lie
ERADICATE	v	abolish	destroy	eliminate	remove
ERRATIC	a	arbitrary	fickle	irregular	unpredictable
ERUDITE	a	educated	knowledgeable	learned	scholarly
ERUDITION	n	education	knowledge	learning	scholarship
ESOTERIC	a	complex	difficult	mysterious	profound
ESPIONAGE	n	intelligence	reconnaissance	spying	surveillance
ESTEEM	n	admiration	honor	regard	respect
ESTIMABLE	a	admirable	good	respectable	worthy
ETHICAL	a	honest	honorable	just	virtuous
ETHICS	n	conscience	morals	principles	standards
EUPHEMISM	n	alternative	expression	saying	substitution
EUPHONY	n	consonance	harmony	melody	tune
EVADE	v	avoid	dodge	elude	escape
EVANESCENT	a	brief	fleeting	short-lived	temporary
EVASIVE	a	elusive	deceitful	shifty	sly
EVOCATIVE	a	expressive	remindful	reminiscent	suggestive
EVOLUTION	n	expansion	development	growth	progression
EXACERBATE	v	aggravate	annoy	intensify	worsen
EXALTED	a	elevated	grand	noble	lofty
EXASPERATE	v	annoy	irritate	provoke	vex
EXCEPTIONAL	a	extraordinary	singular	unique	unusual
EXCLUSIVE	a	elite	private	restricted	special
EXEGESIS	n	clarification	explanation	exposition	interpretation
EXEMPLARY	a	admirable	commendable	model	outstanding
EXEMPLIFY	v	illustrate	represent	symbolize	typify

EXERT	v	apply	exercise	utilize	wield
EXHAUSTIVE	a	complete	comprehensive	detailed	thorough
EXONERATE	v	absolve	acquit	clear	excuse
EXORBITANT	a	excessive	expensive	extravagant	outrageous
EXOTIC	a	foreign	outlandish	strange	unusual
EXPANSE	n	area	extent	range	space
EXPEDIENT	a	advantageous	convenient	opportune	useful
EXPEDITE	v	accelerate	facilitate	hasten	quicken
EXPERTISE	n	ability	knowledge	skill	proficiency
EXPLICIT	a	clear	definite	exact	plain
EXPLOIT	v	abuse	control	manipulate	use
EXPLOIT	n	accomplishment	achievement	deed	feat
EXPOUND	v	clarify	explain	elaborate	illustrate
EXQUISITE	a	beautiful	elegant	excellent	lovely
EXTANT	a	alive	current	existing	present
EXTOL	v	commend	exalt	glorify	praise
EXTRACT	v	pull	remove	uproot	withdraw
EXTRACURRICULAR	a	adulterous	extramarital	external	outside
EXTRANEOUS	a	extra	irrelevant	unimportant	unnecessary
EXTRAVAGANT	a	excessive	extreme	lavish	outrageous
EXULTANT	a	delighted	elated	happy	joyful
EXULTATION	n	elation	joy	rejoicing	triumph
FABRICATE	v	construct	make	manufacture	invent
FACADE	n	disguise	face	false	mask
FACETIOUS	a	humorous	joking	sarcastic	witty
FACILITATE	v	aid	assist	ease	expedite
FACSIMILE	n	copy	duplicate	replica	reproduction
FACULTY	n	ability	aptitude	capacity	talent
FANATIC	n	devotee	enthusiast	extremist	fiend
FANATICAL	a	enthusiastic	fervent	passionate	zealous
FAR-FETCHED	a	doubtful	improbable	unbelievable	unlikely
FARCICAL	a	absurd	funny	laughable	ridiculous
FASTIDIOUS	a	finicky	fussy	meticulous	particular
FATHOM	v	comprehend	grasp	see	understand
FATUOUS	a	asinine	foolish	silly	stupid
FEIGN	v	counterfeit	fake	pretend	simulate
FEISTY	a	lively	ornery	spunky	touchy
FELICITOUS	a	appropriate	fitting	fortunate	opportune
FERTILE	a	fruitful	productive	abundant	plentiful
FERVENT	a	ardent	passionate	vehement	zealous
FERVID	a	ardent	fervent	passionate	zealous
FERVOR	n	enthusiasm	excitement	intensity	passion
FETID	a	odorous	rancid	rank	stinking

FIASCO	n	debacle	disaster	failure	flop
FICKLE	a	changeable	erratic	inconstant	unpredictable
FIDELITY	n	allegiance	devotion	faithfulness	loyalty
FITFUL	a	erratic	intermittent	irregular	spasmodic
FLAGRANT	a	blatant	glaring	heinous	outrageous
FLAMBOYANT	a	extravagant	flashy	gaudy	showy
FLORID	a	flamboyant	flowery	ornate	showy
FLOURISH	v	grow	prosper	succeed	thrive
FLUID	a	flowing	fluent	liquid	unstable
FOOLHARDY	a	daring	hasty	rash	reckless
FORBIDDING	a	grim	hostile	menacing	unfriendly
FORGE	v	construct	fabricate	make	shape
FORGERY	n	counterfeit	fake	imitation	sham
FORMIDABLE	a	fearful	frightful	intimidating	powerful
FORTHRIGHT	a	candid	direct	frank	straightforward
FORTUITOUS	a	accidental	chance	fortunate	lucky
FRUGAL	a	economical	sparing	stingy	thrifty
FRUITFUL	a	fertile	productive	profitable	prolific
FRUITLESS	a	barren	unproductive	futile	useless
FUNDAMENTAL	a	basic	elementary	essential	primary
FURTIVE	a	sly	sneaky	secretive	underhand
FUTILE	a	fruitless	hopeless	ineffective	useless
GALVANIZE	v	animate	arouse	excite	stimulate
GARISH	a	flashy	gaudy	glaring	showy
GARRULOUS	a	chatty	gabby	rambling	talkative
GAUDY	a	flamboyant	flashy	loud	showy
GENTEEL	a	courteous	polite	refined	sophisticated
GERMANE	a	appropriate	fitting	relevant	suitable
GHASTLY	a	frightful	grisly	gruesome	horrible
GIDDY	a	dizzy	flighty	frivolous	unsteady
GIRTH	n	belt	cinch	circumference	perimeter
GLORIFY	v	exalt	praise	revere	worship
GLUM	a	depressed	gloomy	melancholy	sad
GRANDEUR	n	gloriousness	magnificence	majesty	splendidness
GRANDILOQUENT	a	bombastic	grandiose	lofty	pompous
GRANDIOSE	a	lofty	magnificent	pompous	pretentious
GRAPPLE	v	clutch	grasp	struggle	wrestle
GRATIFY	v	delight	indulge	please	satisfy
GRAVE	a	serious	severe	solemn	weighty
GRAVITY	n	importance	seriousness	significance	solemnity
GREGARIOUS	a	friendly	genial	outgoing	sociable
GRIMACE	v	frown	glare	scowl	sneer
GROTESQUE	a	hideous	monstrous	ugly	weird

GUILE	n	craftiness	cunning	deception	trickery
GUISE	n	appearance	pretense	semblance	show
GULLIBLE	a	deceived	fooled	naive	simple
HACKNEYED	a	commonplace	stock	overused	stale
HALCYON	a	calm	peaceful	serene	tranquil
HAMPER	v	block	hinder	impede	obstruct
HAPHAZARD	a	chance	erratic	irregular	random
HARASS	v	annoy	irritate	pester	torment
HARMONIOUS	a	agreeable	congenial	compatible	sympathetic
HAUGHTY	a	arrogant	conceited	proud	snobbish
HEADLONG	a	hasty	impetuous	rash	reckless
HEDONIST	n	deviant	exhibitionist	immoralist	misbehaver
HEDONISTIC	a	depraved	indulgent	luxurious	sensual
HEED	v	follow	regard	notice	observe
HEIR	n	beneficiary	descendant	inheritor	successor
HERESY	n	apostasy	blasphemy	nonconformity	unorthodoxy
HETEROGENEOUS	a	dissimilar	diverse	mixed	varied
HIDEBOUND	a	inflexible	rigid	intolerant	narrow-minded
HINDRANCE	n	barrier	obstruction	interference	restriction
HISTRIONIC	a	affected	artificial	dramatic	theatric
HOARD	n	accumulation	cache	stockpile	store
HOAX	n	deception	fraud	swindle	trick
HOSTILE	a	aggressive	antagonistic	hateful	unfriendly
HYPOCRITICAL	a	deceitful	dishonest	false	insincere
HYPOTHESIS	n	assumption	conjecture	guess	theory
HYPOTHETICAL	a	speculative	theoretical	uncertain	unproven
ICONOCLASTIC	a	dissenting	nonconformist	radical	unconventional
IDEOLOGICAL	a	abstract	conceptual	mental	theoretical
IDIOM	n	dialect	jargon	expression	phrase
IDIOSYNCRASY	n	characteristic	distinctive	odd	peculiarity
ILL-CONCEIVED	a	absurd	foolish	half-baked	misguided
ILLEGIBLE	a	indecipherable	obscure	unclear	unreadable
ILLICIT	a	criminal	illegal	illegitimate	unlawful
ILLUMINATE	v	brighten	lighten	explain	illustrate
ILLUSTRIOUS	a	celebrated	distinguished	famous	notable
IMMACULATE	a	clean	spotless	faultless	pure
IMMINENT	a	approaching	impending	close	near
IMMORTALITY	n	afterlife	deathlessness	eternity	hereafter
IMMUNE	a	persistent	resistant	stable	strong
IMMUTABLE	a	constant	fixed	permanent	unchangeable
IMPART	v	bestow	give	convey	reveal
IMPARTIAL	a	disinterested	fair	neutral	unbiased
IMPASSE	n	deadlock	predicament	standstill	stalemate

IMPASSIVE	a	calm	cool	unconcerned	unemotional
IMPECCABLE	a	faultless	flawless	immaculate	perfect
IMPEDE	v	block	hinder	obstruct	stop
IMPEDIMENT	n	barrier	hindrance	obstacle	obstruction
IMPENDING	a	approaching	coming	close	forthcoming
IMPERATIVE	a	essential	necessary	pressing	vital
IMPERIOUS	a	arrogant	dictatorial	domineering	overbearing
IMPERMEABLE	a	impenetrable	impervious	compact	tight
IMPERVIOUS	a	impassable	impenetrable	impermeable	resistant
IMPETUOUS	a	hasty	impulsive	overeager	rash
IMPLAUSIBLE	a	improbable	inconceivable	unbelievable	unlikely
IMPLICATE	v	concern	entangle	incriminate	involve
IMPLICATION	n	connotation	indication	meaning	significance
IMPLY	v	hint	indicate	mean	suggest
IMPOSING	a	grand	impressive	intimidating	majestic
IMPOVERISHED	a	broke	destitute	needy	poor
IMPREGNABLE	a	firm	hard	invincible	strong
IMPRESSIONABLE	a	receptive	responsive	sensitive	susceptible
IMPROBABLE	a	doubtful	incredible	questionable	unlikely
IMPROMPTU	a	improvise	offhand	spontaneous	unprepared
IMPROPRIETY	n	improperness	indecency	mistake	unfitness
IMPRUDENCE	n	carelessness	indiscretion	rashness	recklessness
IMPRUDENT	a	careless	rash	reckless	thoughtless
IMPULSIVE	a	hasty	rash	reckless	spontaneous
INADVERTENT	a	careless	inattentive	negligent	thoughtless
INANE	a	absurd	foolish	silly	stupid
INAUDIBLE	a	faint	imperceptible	quiet	unhearable
INCANTATION	n	chant	charm	magic	spell
INCARCERATE	v	confine	detain	imprison	jail
INCESSANT	a	constant	continuous	relentless	unceasing
INCOHERENT	a	confused	disconnected	disjointed	rambling
INCOMPETENT	a	inadequate	incapable	ineffective	inefficient
INCOMPREHENSIBLE	a	mysterious	obscure	unfathomable	unintelligible
INCONCEIVABLE	a	impossible	incredible	unimaginable	unthinkable
INCONCLUSIVE	a	indecisive	indeterminate	uncertain	weak
INCONGRUOUS	a	absurd	inappropriate	inconstant	unsuitable
INCONSPICUOUS	a	faint	insignificant	obscure	unobtrusive
INCONTROVERTIBLE	a	irredeemable	obstinate	unmanageable	unreformable
INCORRIGIBLE	a	incurable	stubborn	uncontrollable	unruly
INCREDULOUS	a	disbelieving	distrustful	skeptical	suspicious
INDECISION	n	doubt	fluctuation	hesitation	uncertainty
INDEFATIGABLE	a	determined	persistent	steadfast	untiring
INDELIBLE	a	indestructible	lasting	permanent	unerasable

INDETERMINATE	a	indefinite	indistinct	uncertain	vague
INDIFFERENCE	n	apathy	coolness	disinterest	unconcern
INDIFFERENT	a	apathetic	cool	neutral	unconcerned
INDIGNATION	n	anger	displeasure	fury	resentment
INDISTINCT	a	blurry	unclear	indefinite	vague
INDOLENCE	n	idleness	inactivity	laziness	sluggishness
INDOMITABLE	a	brave	determined	invincible	unconquerable
INDULGE	v	coddle	gratify	pamper	spoil
INDULGENT	a	easygoing	kind	lenient	tolerant
INDUSTRIOUS	a	busy	diligent	energetic	hard-working
INEFFECTUAL	a	futile	ineffective	unavailing	useless
INERT	a	idle	inactive	sluggish	unreactive
INEVITABLE	a	certain	destined	inescapable	unavoidable
INEXORABLE	a	inflexible	merciless	relentless	unyielding
INFALLIBLE	a	certain	reliable	sure	unerring
INFAMOUS	a	disreputable	notorious	scandalous	villainous
INFER	v	conclude	deduce	gather	guess
INFERRED	a	deduced	implied	presumed	understood
INGENIOUS	a	clever	cunning	intelligent	inventive
INGENUITY	n	ability	cleverness	skill	talent
INGENUOUS	a	candid	frank	honest	straightforward
INHERENT	a	built-in	inborn	ingrained	natural
INHIBITION	n	hindrance	impediment	restraint	restriction
INIMITABLE	a	matchless	peerless	unparalleled	unrivaled
INIQUITY	n	evil	injustice	sin	wickedness
INITIAL	a	first	introductory	opening	original
INITIATE	v	begin	commence	originate	start
INITIATIVE	n	ambition	drive	energy	enterprise
INJURIOUS	a	damaging	destructive	detrimental	harmful
INNATE	a	inborn	inherited	natural	native
INNOCUOUS	a	harmless	innocent	inoffensive	safe
INNOVATE	v	create	introduce	originate	pioneer
INNOVATIVE	a	advanced	groundbreaking	inventive	original
INNUMERABLE	a	countless	incalculable	infinite	numberless
INQUISITIVE	a	curious	inquiring	nosy	questioning
INSATIABLE	a	gluttonous	ravenous	unquenchable	voracious
INSCRUTABLE	a	inexplicable	mysterious	puzzling	unfathomable
INSIDIOUS	a	cunning	deceitful	treacherous	tricky
INSIGHT	n	discernment	perception	understanding	wisdom
INSIGNIFICANT	a	inconsequential	minor	trivial	unimportant
INSINUATION	n	hint	suggestion	implication	slur
INSIPID	a	bland	dull	tedious	uninteresting
INSOLENT	a	brazen	disrespectful	insulting	rude

INSTIGATE	v	incite	inspire	prompt	provoke
INSULATED	a	divided	isolated	segregated	separate
INTACT	a	entire	complete	unbroken	whole
INTEGRAL	a	built-in	hardwired	all-important	essential
INTEGRATE	v	combine	incorporate	unify	unite
INTEGRITY	n	honesty	morality	uprightness	virtue
INTEMPERATE	a	excessive	extreme	immoderate	unrestrained
INTERROGATION	n	examination	inquiry	investigation	question
INTERVENE	v	interfere	interrupt	meddle	mediate
INTOLERANCE	n	fanaticism	narrow-mindedness	opinionatedness	partiality
INTRACTABLE	a	inflexible	stubborn	unmanageable	unruly
INTREPID	a	bold	brave	courageous	fearless
INTRICACY	n	complexity	difficulty	entanglement	involvement
INTRICATE	a	complex	complicated	difficult	involved
INTRIGUE	v	connive	conspire	fascinate	interest
INTRIGUE	n	conspiracy	design	plot	scheme
INTRINSIC	a	inborn	inherent	ingrained	nature
INTUITION	n	feeling	hunch	insight	instinct
INVALUABLE	a	costly	dear	precious	priceless
INVENTIVENESS	n	cleverness	creativity	imagination	ingenuity
INVETERATE	a	confirmed	chronic	deep-rooted	habitual
INVIGORATING	a	energizing	enlivening	exhilarating	stimulating
INVOLUNTARY	a	automatic	instinctive	spontaneous	unconscious
IRASCIBLE	a	cranky	irritable	testy	touchy
IRK	v	annoy	bother	harass	irritate
IRONIC	a	caustic	cynical	sarcastic	wry
IRONY	n	mockery	ridicule	sarcasm	satire
IRRATIONAL	a	absurd	crazy	foolish	illogical
IRRELEVANT	a	immaterial	inapplicable	inappropriate	unrelated
IRREVOCABLE	a	certain	irretrievable	irreversible	unalterable
JARGON	n	lingo	slang	pretentious	specialized
JEOPARDY	n	danger	hazard	peril	risk
JOSTLE	v	elbow	push	shove	bump
JUBILANT	a	delighted	happy	joyful	pleased
JUDICIOUS	a	discreet	prudent	sensible	sound
KEEN	a	acute	sharp	eager	zealous
KINDLE	v	arouse	inspire	provoke	stimulate
LACERATION	n	cut	gash	rip	wound
LACKLUSTER	a	dim	drab	dull	colorless
LAMENTATION	n	grief	mourning	complaint	regret
LAMPOON	v	mock	parody	ridicule	satirize
LANGUID	a	dull	inactive	lazy	sluggish
LANGUISH	v	decline	fade	deteriorate	wither

LARGESS	n	bounty	charity	generosity	goodwill
LATENT	a	concealed	dormant	hidden	inactive
LAUDABLE	a	admirable	commendable	estimable	praiseworthy
LAUGHINGSTOCK	n	dupe	fool	joke	mockery
LAVISH	a	extravagant	luxurious	generous	liberal
LEGACY	n	heritage	inheritance	bequest	gift
LEGIBLE	a	clear	plain	intelligible	readable
LEGITIMATE	a	legal	proper	true	valid
LETHAL	a	deadly	fatal	mortal	poisonous
LETHARGIC	a	drowsy	dull	inactive	sluggish
LETHARGY	n	drowsiness	inactivity	laziness	sluggishness
LEVITY	n	flippancy	frivolity	lightness	silliness
LISTLESS	a	dull	inactive	sluggish	unconcerned
LITERAL	a	accurate	exact	precise	true
LITHE	a	flexible	limber	nimble	supple
LOFTY	a	elevated	exalted	grand	high
LOQUACIOUS	a	chatty	long-winded	talkative	wordy
LUCID	a	intelligible	rational	sane	understandable
LUDICROUS	a	absurd	laughable	ridiculous	preposterous
LURID	a	ghastly	gruesome	sensational	vivid
LUSCIOUS	a	appetizing	delicious	tasty	scrumptious
LUXURIANT	a	abundant	fruitful	lavish	lush
LYRIC	a	ballad	poem	verse	words
MAGNANIMOUS	a	courageous	generous	honorable	noble
MAGNATE	n	baron	mogul	king	tycoon
MAGNITUDE	n	dimension	extent	mass	size
MALCONTENT	a	discontented	disgruntled	dissatisfied	unhappy
MALEVOLENT	a	evil	hateful	malicious	spiteful
MALICIOUS	a	hateful	mean	spiteful	vicious
MALODOROUS	a	foul	putrid	rank	smelly
MANIC	a	crazy	frenzied	insane	mad
MANIFEST	a	clear	evident	obvious	plain
MANIFEST	v	demonstrate	display	reveal	show
MANIPULATE	v	control	handle	manage	operate
MARRED	v	damaged	defaced	disfigured	scarred
MASONRY	n	brickwork	stonework	trade	Freemasonry
MASQUERADE	n	act	front	pretense	show
MASQUERADE	v	disguise	impersonate	pose	pretend
MEAGER	a	lean	scanty	slight	sparse
MEANDER	v	ramble	roam	rove	wander
MEANDERING	a	roundabout	turning	twisting	winding
MEDIATE	v	intercede	referee	negotiate	settle
MEDIOCRITY	n	average	generality	inferiority	medium

MELANCHOLY	a	gloomy	reflective	sad	unhappy
MELODRAMATIC	a	exaggerated	overdone	sensational	theatrical
MERGER	n	blend	combination	fusion	joining
MERITORIOUS	a	admirable	commendable	creditable	praiseworthy
MESMERIZE	v	charm	enchant	fascinate	hypnotize
METAMORPHOSIS	n	alteration	change	mutation	transformation
METAPHORICAL	a	allegorical	comparative	figurative	symbolic
METAPHYSICAL	a	abstract	spiritual	supernatural	unearthly
METHODICAL	a	careful	orderly	regular	systematic
METICULOUS	a	careful	detailed	particular	precise
METTLE	n	bravery	courage	fortitude	nerve
MIGRATE	v	leave	move	relocate	travel
MIME	v	copy	imitate	impersonate	mimic
MINUSCULE	a	little	minute	small	tiny
MINUTE	a	little	microscopic	small	tiny
MISANTHROPE	n	cynic	hater of mankind	man-hater	pessimist
MISAPPREHENSION	n	misconception	misinterpretation	mistake	misunderstanding
MISER		cheapskate	skinflint	Scrooge	tightwad
MISHAP	n	accident	disaster	catastrophe	misfortune
MITIGATE	v	alleviate	ease	lessen	soothe
MOBILITY	n	action	flexibility	motion	movability
MOCK	v	jeer	ridicule	tease	taunt
MOCK	a	artificial	counterfeit	fake	sham
MODERATION	n	frugality	restraint	sobriety	temperance
MODEST	a	humble	shy	unassuming	unpretentious
MONARCH	n	crowned head	king	sovereign	queen
MONARCHY	n	empire	kingdom	realm	sovereignty
MONOLITHIC	a	large	massive	solid	uniform
MONOTONOUS		boring	dull	humdrum	uninteresting
MOROSE	a	depressed	gloomy	glum	sad
MORTIFIED	a	ashamed	embarrassed	humbled	humiliated
MOSAIC	a	checkered	inlayed	patchwork	variegated
MOTIVATE	v	encourage	move	prompt	stimulate
MOTIVATION	n	encouragement	impulse	incentive	stimulus
MOTIVE	n	cause	grounds	rationale	reason
MUNDANE	a	earthly	ordinary	terrestrial	worldly
MUNIFICENCE	n	charity	generosity	liberality	unselfishness
MUSE	n	minstrel	poet	rhymester	versifier
MUSE	v	consider	contemplate	meditate	ponder
MYRIAD	n	abundance	boatload	heap	multitude
MYRIAD	a	countless	infinite	innumerable	numberless
NAIVE	a	candid	gullible	innocent	unsophisticated
NEFARIOUS	a	evil	vile	villainous	wicked

NEGATE	v	cancel	contradict	deny	refute
NEGLIGENCE	n	carelessness	dereliction	inattention	oversight
NEGLIGIBLE	a	insignificant	trifling	trivial	unimportant
NEUTRAL	a	detached	impartial	objective	unbiased
NICHE	n	alcove	corner	nook	recess
NONCHALANT	a	apathetic	casual	disinterested	unconcerned
NONDESCRIPT	a	characterless	common	dull	ordinary
NOSTALGIA	n	homesickness	longing	sentimentality	yearning
NOTABLE	a	distinguished	noteworthy	outstanding	prominent
NOTEWORTHY	a	extraordinary	important	outstanding	remarkable
NOTORIOUS	a	disreputable	infamous	renowned	well-known
NOVEL	a	fresh	new	original	unique
NOVELTY	n	freshness	innovation	newness	originality
NOVICE	n	amateur	apprentice	beginner	greenhorn
NOXIOUS	a	foul	harmful	poisonous	toxic
NULLIFY	v	cancel	invalidate	neutralize	void
NURTURE	v	foster	nourish	nurse	sustain
OBDURATE	v	determined	stubborn	uncompromising	unyielding
OBFUSCATION	n	bafflement	bewilderment	mystification	puzzlement
OBJECTIVE	n	aim	goal	purpose	target
OBJECTIVE	a	fair	impartial	unbiased	unprejudiced
OBLIQUE	a	devious	crooked	indirect	roundabout
OBLITERATE	v	delete	destroy	eliminate	erase
OBLIVIOUS	a	clueless	ignorant	inattentive	unaware
OBSCURE	a	dark	dim	unclear	vague
OBSCURE	v	cloak	cloud	conceal	hide
OBSEQUIOUS	a	fawning	obedient	submissive	subservient
OBSESSIVE	a	compulsive	fanatic	fixated	passionate
OBSOLETE	a	ancient	antiquated	old-fashioned	outdated
OBSTINATE	a	adamant	inflexible	stubborn	unyielding
OBTUSE	a	dense	dumb	slow	stupid
OCCULT	a	cryptic	obscure	mysterious	secret
OFFENSIVE	a	disgusting	foul	nasty	repulsive
OFFICIOUS	a	intrusive	meddlesome	nosy	prying
OMINOUS	a	grim	menacing	sinister	threatening
OMNISCIENT	a	all knowing	almighty	divine	wise
ONEROUS	a	burdensome	difficult	hard	oppressive
OPAQUE	a	cloudy	hazy	murky	unclear
OPPRESSIVE	a	burdensome	cruel	severe	tough
OPULENT	a	luxurious	prosperous	rich	wealthy
ORACLE	n	prophet	seer	soothsayer	vision
ORATOR	n	talker	lecturer	speaker	spokesman
ORATORY	n	diction	elocution	rhetoric	public speaking

ORDEAL	n	distress	torment	trial	tribulation
ORNATE	a	baroque	elaborate	fancy	rococo
ORTHODOX	a	conventional	established	standard	traditional
OSCILLATE	v	fluctuate	sway	vibrate	waver
OSTENTATIOUS	a	extravagant	gaudy	pretentious	showy
OUTLANDISH	a	bizarre	eccentric	odd	strange
OVERT	a	clear	obvious	open	unconcealed
OVERWROUGHT	a	excited	frantic	nervous	upset
PAINSTAKING	a	careful	conscientious	fussy	thorough
PALLID	a	ashen	bloodless	pale	sallow
PALTRY	a	insignificant	negligible	trivial	unimportant
PANORAMIC	a	beautiful	comprehensive	scenic	wide
PARADOX	n	absurdity	contradiction	inconsistency	puzzle
PARAGON	n	champion	ideal	model	standard
PARAPHRASE	v	explain	interpret	restate	reword
PAROCHIAL	a	limited	local	narrow	regional
PARSIMONY	n	economy	frugality	stinginess	thrift
PASTICHE	n	copy	imitation	medley	potpourri
PATENT	a	apparent	clear	evident	obvious
PATRONIZING	a	arrogant	condescending	snobbish	snooty
PAUCITY	n	insufficiency	lack	scarcity	shortage
PECCADILLO	n	fault	flaw	indiscretion	offense
PEDANT	n	bookworm	formalist	perfectionist	purist
PEDESTAL	n	base	foundation	stand	support
PEDESTRIAN	a	commonplace	dull	humdrum	ordinary
PENCHANT	n	inclination	fondness	leaning	liking
PENSIVE	a	contemplative	meditative	reflective	thoughtful
PENURY	n	destitution	need	poverty	want
PERCEIVE	v	discern	see	sense	understand
PERCEPTION	n	awareness	discernment	insight	understanding
PERCEPTIVE	a	discerning	keen	sharp	wise
PERENNIAL	a	continual	lasting	permanent	perpetual
PERFUNCTORY	a	careless	negligent	mechanical	routine
PERIPHERAL	a	boundary	external	outer	outlying
PERIPHERY	n	border	boundary	edge	perimeter
PERJURE	v	deceive	falsify	fib	lie
PERNICIOUS	a	deadly	destructive	fatal	ruinous
PERORATION	a	conclusion	end	finale	oration
PERSECUTION	n	abuse	oppression	torment	torture
PERSISTENT	a	consistent	firm	stable	strong
PERSPICACIOUS	a	discerning	keen	perceptive	wise
PERTINENT	a	applicable	appropriate	fitting	relevant
PERTURBATION	n	agitation	commotion	disturbance	fluster

PERUSE	v	examine	read	scrutinize	study
PERVADE	v	fill	penetrate	permeate	saturate
PERVERSE	a	contrary	obstinate	stubborn	wayward
PERVERT	v	corrupt	distort	misrepresent	warp
PETRIFIED	a	afraid	horrified	paralyzed	terrified
PETTY	a	insignificant	mean	small	unimportant
PHENOMENA	n	curiosities	miracles	oddities	rarities
PHILANTHROPIST	n	donor	humanitarian	patron	supporter
PHILANTHROPY	n	charity	generosity	goodwill	kindness
PHILISTINE	n	barbarian	rude	uncivilized	uncultured
PHLEGMATIC	a	calm	cool	sluggish	unemotional
PIONEER	v	establish	found	initiate	originate
PIOUS	a	devout	holy	religious	reverent
PIVOTAL	a	critical	crucial	important	momentous
PLACID	a	calm	peaceful	quiet	still
PLAGIARIST	n	copycat	imitator	parrot	pirate
PLATEAU	n	highland	level	plain	tableland
PLAUSIBLE	a	believable	credible	probable	reasonable
PLENTITUDE	n	abundance	affluence	bountifulness	wealth
PLETHORA	n	excess	overabundance	oversupply	surplus
PODIUM	n	pulpit	stand	platform	stage
POIGNANT	a	biting	penetrating	piercing	sharp
POISED	a	balanced	calm	collected	composed
POMPOUS	a	affected	arrogant	haughty	pretentious
PONDEROUS	a	bulky	heavy	massive	weighty
PORTLY	a	fat	heavy	obese	stout
PORTRAY	v	depict	describe	draw	represent
POSTHUMOUS	a	after death	postmortem	belated	delayed
POTENT	a	forceful	influential	powerful	strong
PRAGMATIC	a	realistic	reasonable	practical	sensible
PRECARIOUS	a	dangerous	hazardous	risky	sensitive
PRECEPT	n	decree	law	principle	rule
PRECIPITATE	v	accelerate	cause	hasten	quicken
PRECIPITATE	a	abrupt	hasty	rash	sudden
PRECLUDE	v	exclude	hinder	prevent	prohibit
PRECONCEIVED	a	biased	deliberate	intentional	premeditated
PREDECESSOR	n	ancestor	forefather	forerunner	parent
PREDETERMINED	a	destined	fated	fixed	foreordained
PREDILECTION	n	fondness	inclination	partiality	preference
PREDOMINANT	a	chief	dominant	leading	superior
PREEMINENT	a	chief	dominant	prominent	supreme
PRELIMINARY	a	introductory	preceding	preparatory	prior
PREMONITION	n	prediction	prophecy	sign	warning

PREPOSTEROUS	a	absurd	foolish	ridiculous	silly
PREREQUISITE	n	essential	imperative	necessity	requirement
PRESCIENT	a	foreknowable	foresighted	prophetic	provident
PRESCRIBE	v	decree	dictate	ordain	order
PRESTIGIOUS	a	celebrated	distinguished	notable	respected
PRESUMPTUOUS	a	assuming	bold	brazen	forward
PRETENTIOUS	a	affected	arrogant	haughty	inflated
PREVAIL	v	dominate	overcome	triumph	win
PREVAILING	a	common	current	popular	widespread
PREVALENT	a	common	general	usual	widespread
PREVARICATE	v	evade	dodge	fib	lie
PRIMORDIAL	a	early	original	primal	primitive
PRIORITY	n	order	preference	rank	urgency
PROBLEMATIC	a	complicated	difficult	tricky	questionable
PROCRASTINATE	v	delay	linger	postpone	stall
PROCURE	v	acquire	get	obtain	secure
PRODDING	n	goading	prompting	spurring	urging
PRODIGAL	a	extravagant	spendthrift	squanderer	wasteful
PRODIGIOUS	a	enormous	extraordinary	immense	monumental
PROFICIENT	a	accomplished	competent	expert	skillful
PROFOUND	a	deep	difficult	insightful	knowledgeable
PROFUSE	a	abundant	lavish	luxuriant	plentiful
PROFUSION	n	abundance	excess	plenty	wealth
PROGNOSIS	n	forecast	prediction	projection	prophecy
PROLIFIC	a	abundant	fertile	fruitful	productive
PROMINENT	a	celebrated	distinguished	notable	outstanding
PROMONTORY	n	cape	foreland	headland	hill
PROMULGATE	v	broadcast	disseminate	proclaim	publish
PRONE	a	apt	inclined	liable	predisposed
PROPENSITY	n	bias	inclination	leaning	tendency
PROPHETIC	a	fateful	foreshadowing	predictive	telling
PROPOSAL	n	plan	proposition	scheme	suggestion
PROPOUND	v	advance	offer	propose	submit
PROPRIETY	n	correctness	decency	fitness	properness
PROSAIC	a	boring	dull	ordinary	uninteresting
PROSPERITY	n	affluence	fortune	success	wealth
PROSPEROUS	a	affluent	flourishing	rich	wealthy
PROTAGONIST	n	champion	defender	fighter	hero
PROTOTYPE	n	model	original	pattern	standard
PROTRACTED	a	drawn-out	extended	lengthy	long
PROTRUDING	a	bulge	jutting	projecting	prominent
PROVERBIAL	a	familiar	famous	notorious	well-known
PROVINCIAL	a	country	local	regional	rustic

PROVOCATIVE	a	exciting	seductive	sexy	stimulating
PROVOKE	v	annoy	arouse	incite	irritate
PRUDENT	a	careful	cautious	discreet	wise
PRURIENT	a	carnal	lewd	lustful	sexy
PSEUDONYM	n	alias	disguise	incognito	nickname
PUGILIST	n	battler	boxer	combatant	fighter
PUNGENT	a	acrid	biting	penetrating	sharp
PURGATION	n	cleaning	clearing	evacuation	purification
PURLOIN	v	lift	rob	steal	swipe
PURPORT	v	allege	claim	profess	signify
QUAGMIRE	n	dilemma	predicament	marsh	swamp
QUANDARY	n	dilemma	perplexity	predicament	uncertainty
QUARRY	n	game	prey	target	victim
QUERULOUS	a	complaining	cross	irritable	testy
QUIBBLE	v	bicker	dispute	dodge	evade
QUIESCENT	a	motionless	quiet	still	tranquil
QUIZZICAL	a	bantering	jesting	joking	kidding
RACONTEUR	n	narrator	novelist	spinner of yarns	storyteller
RADICAL	a	extreme	fanatical	rabid	revolutionary
RADICAL	n	crazy	extremist	fanatic	revolutionist
RANDOM	a	casual	chance	haphazard	irregular
RASH	a	brash	hasty	foolhardy	reckless
RATIONAL	a	intelligent	logical	reasonable	sound
RATIONALIST	n	functionalism	positivist	realist	reasonableness
RAUCOUS	a	harsh	hoarse	rough	strident
RAVAGE	n	demolish	destroy	ruin	plunder
REBUT	v	answer	deny	disprove	refute
REBUTTAL	n	answer	counter argument	reply	response
RECALCITRANT	a	defiant	disobedient	stubborn	unruly
RECANT	v	recall	retract	revoke	withdraw
RECIPROCATE	v	exchange	interchange	retaliate	return
RECKONING	n	account	calculation	computation	tally
RECLUSE	n	hermit	loner	outcast	solitary
RECONCILE	v	adjust	balance	resolve	settle
RECOUNT	v	narrate	recite	relate	tell
RECTIFY	v	correct	improve	remedy	repair
RECTITUDE	n	honesty	integrity	uprightness	virtue
RECUPERATE	v	convalesce	heal	improve	recover
REDUNDANT	a	excess	extra	repetitive	unnecessary
REFINEMENT	n	cultivation	culture	elegance	sophistication
REFLECTIVE	a	meditative	pondering	thinking	thoughtful
REFUTE	v	deny	disprove	contradict	rebut
REGAL	a	grand	imperial	majestic	royal

REGULATE	v	adjust	control	direct	manage
REIGN	v	command	dominate	govern	rule
REITERATION	n	echo	frequency	recurrence	repetition
REJUVENATE	v	refresh	renew	restore	revive
REJUVENATED	v	enlivened	mended	refreshed	restored
REJUVENATING	a	enlivening	exhilarating	invigorating	refreshing
RELATIVE	a	applicable	pertinent	proportionate	related
RELEGATE	v	banish	demote	dismiss	transfer
RELENT	v	give in	let up	slacken	yield
RELEVANT	a	applicable	appropriate	fitting	proper
RELIC	n	antique	keepsake	memento	souvenir
RELUCTANCE	n	doubt	hesitation	misgiving	unwillingness
REMINISCENCE	n	memory	recall	recollection	retrospection
REMINISCENT	a	nostalgic	recalling	remindful	suggestive
REMONSTRATE	v	disapprove	except	object	protest
REMORSE	n	guilt	regret	sadness	sorrow
RENEGADE	a	deserter	rebel	traitor	turncoat
RENOUNCE	v	abandon	disown	forsake	relinquish
RENOVATE	v	refurbish	recondition	repair	restore
RENOWN	n	celebrity	distinction	fame	reputation
RENOWNED	a	celebrated	eminent	famous	illustrious
REPEAL	v	abolish	cancel	recall	revoke
REPERTOIRE	n	capabilities	masteries	proficiencies	talents
REPREHENSIBLE	a	abominable	blameworthy	disgraceful	shameful
REPRESS	v	restrain	stifle	subdue	suppress
REPRESSION	n	control	restraint	oppression	suppression
REPRESSIVE	a	arrogant	domineering	overbearing	restrictive
REPRIMAND	n	denunciation	lecture	rebuke	scold
REPROACH	v	blame	rebuke	reprimand	scold
REPROACHFUL	a	accusatory	critical	disapproving	disparaging
REPROBATE	n	corrupt	degenerate	unprincipled	wicked
REPUDIATE	v	deny	disown	refuse	reject
REPUGNANT	a	disgusting	offensive	repulsive	revolting
RESCIND	v	cancel	repeal	revoke	void
RESENTMENT	n	anger	bitterness	hostility	spite
RESIDUAL	a	balance	leftover	remaining	surplus
RESIGNATION	n	abandonment	relinquishment	submission	surrender
RESILIENT	a	hard	persistent	stiff	strong
RESOLUTE	a	determined	resolved	settled	steadfast
RESONANT	a	booming	resounding	reverberating	vibrant
RESOURCEFUL	a	clever	inventive	sharp	skillful
RESPITE	n	break	pause	relief	rest
RESTRAIN	v	control	hinder	restrict	suppress

RESTRAINT	n	confinement	constraint	hindrance	restriction
RETICENT	a	reserved	restrained	shy	uncommunicative
RETORT	n	answer	comeback	reply	response
RETRACT	v	cancel	recall	revoke	withdraw
RETROSPECT	n	flashback	recollection	remembering	review
REVEL	v	celebrate	delight	frolic	rejoice
REVELATION	n	disclosure	discovery	foreshadowing	prophecy
REVERE	v	adore	respect	reverence	worship
REVERENCE	n	admiration	esteem	respect	worship
REVITALIZE	v	refresh	rejuvenate	renew	revive
RHETORIC	n	elocution	oratory	speech	address
RIBALD	a	coarse	gross	indecent	vulgar
RIDICULE	n	contempt	mockery	sarcasm	scorn
RIGOROUS	a	exact	harsh	severe	strict
RITUAL	n	ceremony	custom	formality	rite
RIVALRY	n	competition	conflict	contention	contest
ROBUST	a	persistent	sound	strong	vigorous
ROTUND	a	fat	obese	plump	round
RUDIMENT	n	base	basic	element	fundamental
RUEFUL	a	mournful	regretful	sad	sorry
RUMINATE	v	contemplate	meditate	ponder	reflect
RUTHLESS	a	brutal	cruel	merciless	savage
SABOTAGE	v	destroy	wreck	subvert	undermine
SACCHARINE	a	sentimental	sugary	sweet	syrupy
SAGACIOUS	a	discerning	insightful	perceptive	shrewd
SAGE	a	intelligent	judicious	sensible	wise
SALIENT	a	notable	noticeable	prominent	remarkable
SALLOW	a	ashen	pale	pasty	sickly
SALUBRIOUS	a	beneficial	favorable	healthful	wholesome
SALUTARY	a	beneficial	good	healthful	wholesome
SANCTION	v	approve	authorize	endorse	support
SANCTUARY	n	haven	refuge	retreat	shelter
SARCASM	n	irony	mockery	satire	ridicule
SATIATE	v	gratify	satisfy	gorge	quench
SATIRICAL	a	biting	cutting	cynical	mocking
SAUNTER	v	ramble	stroll	hike	tromp
SAVANT	n	authority	expert	intellectual	scholar
SAVOR	v	appreciate	enjoy	like	taste
SCANTY	a	inadequate	meager	scarce	sparse
SCATTERBRAINED	a	flighty	frivolous	giddy	silly
SCINTILLATING	a	brilliant	gleaming	glittering	sparkling
SCOPE	n	area	extent	range	reach
SCOUNDREL	n	rascal	rogue	cheat	swindler

SCRUPLE	n	doubt	hesitation	misgiving	uncertainty
SCRUPULOUS	a	careful	conscientious	principled	strict
SCRUTINIZE	v	examine	inspect	investigate	study
SCURRILOUS	a	abusive	coarse	insulting	vulgar
SECLUDED	a	isolated	remote	lonely	solitary
SECT	n	denomination	faction	faith	group
SEDUCE	v	allure	beguile	entice	tempt
SELF-AGGRANDIZEMENT	n	arrogance	boastfulness	conceit	egotism
SENILE	a	aged	old	decrepit	infirm
SENTIMENT	n	attitude	feeling	opinion	view
SENTIMENTAL	a	emotional	mushy	romantic	tender
SENTINEL	n	guard	lookout	sentry	watchman
SERENE	a	calm	composed	cool	peaceful
SERENITY	n	calmness	composure	peacefulness	quietness
SERPENTINE	a	crooked	curved	snaky	winding
SERVILE	a	humble	slavish	submissive	subservient
SHARD	n	fragment	piece	scrap	sliver
SHREWD	a	clever	crafty	cunning	sharp
SHROUD	n	blanket	cloak	covering	veil
SHROUDED	a	concealed	hidden	obscure	secret
SHUN	v	avoid	dodge	eschew	reject
SIMULTANEOUS	a	coincident	concurrent	contemporary	synchronous
SINGULAR	a	extraordinary	peculiar	unique	unusual
SINUOUS	a	complex	complicated	intricate	winding
SKEPTICAL	a	disbelieving	distrustful	doubting	suspicious
SLANDER	v	defame	malign	slur	smear
SLOTHFUL	a	idle	inactive	lazy	sluggish
SLUGGISH	a	inactive	lazy	slow	plodding
SMIRK	v	simper	sneer	snicker	leer
SMUG	a	conceited	proud	self-satisfied	vain
SOBRIETY	n	abstinence	composed	gravity	moderation
SOJOURN	v	abide	crash	dwell	lodge
SOJOURN	n	stay	stopover	visit	vacation
SOLEMN	a	dignified	grave	serious	somber
SOLICIT	v	beg	implore	petition	request
SOLICITOUS	a	attentive	careful	concerned	considerate
SOLIDARITY	n	accord	harmony	oneness	unity
SOLITUDE	n	isolation	loneliness	privacy	seclusion
SOMBER	a	anxious	attentive	concerned	thoughtful
SONOROUS	a	full	majestic	resonant	rich sounding
SOOTHSAYER	n	fortune-teller	oracle	prophet	seer
SOPHISTICATED	a	complex	complicated	cultured	refined
SOPHOMORIC	a	childish	foolish	immature	young

SOPORIFIC	a	drowsy	narcotic	opiate	sleepy
SORDID	a	dirty	foul	dishonorable	sleazy
SPARSE	a	poor	scanty	scarce	thin
SPARTAN	a	disciplined	harsh	severe	stern
SPECIFICITY	n	accuracy	explicitness	particularity	peculiarity
SPECIFY	v	define	determine	indicate	name
SPECTRAL	a	eerie	ghostly	supernatural	unearthly
SPECULATE	v	hypothesize	ponder	suppose	theorize
SPECULATION	n	guess	hypothesis	supposition	venture
SPECULATOR	n	gambler	gamester	investor	operator
SPENDTHRIFT	n	extravagancy	spender	squanderer	waster
SPONTANEOUS	a	extemporaneous	impulsive	involuntary	natural
SPURIOUS	a	artificial	bogus	counterfeit	false
SQUABBLE	n	dispute	fight	quarrel	spat
SQUANDER	v	blow	spend	throw away	waste
SQUANDERING	a	extravagant	lavish	unthrifty	wasteful
STAGNANT	a	motionless	stationary	stale	foul
STAGNATION	n	inactivity	motionless	doldrums	slump
STAID	a	sedate	serious	sober	solemn
STALWART	a	robust	strong	stout	sturdy
STANZA	n	division	section	text	verse
STATELY	a	grand	imposing	majestic	noble
STATIC	a	inactive	immobile	stationary	unchanging
STATURE	n	importance	quality	rank	standing
STATUS	n	condition	position	rank	standing
STAUNCH	a	faithful	firm	loyal	steadfast
STEADFAST	a	firm	persistent	stable	steady
STEREOTYPE	v	catalogue	categorize	define	stamp
STIMULATE	v	animate	arouse	excite	stir
STIMULUS	n	incentive	incitement	inducement	provocation
STOIC	a	apathetic	unaffected	unemotional	unresponsive
STRATAGEM	n	ploy	ruse	scheme	trick
STRATUM	n	layer	level	plane	rank
STRIDENT	a	discordant	harsh	loud	shrill
STRIVE	v	attempt	contend	endeavor	toil
STUDIOUS	a	bookish	diligent	industrious	scholarly
STUPEFACTION	n	amazement	bewilderment	surprise	wonder
STUPEFY	v	amaze	astonish	dumfound	stun
STYLIZED	a	amplified	abstract	beautiful	elegant
SUAVE	a	suave	refined	smooth	sophisticated
SUBDUED	a	muted	quiet	restrained	soft
SUBJECTIVE	a	emotional	individualize	instinctive	personalized
SUBORDINATE	a	inferior	junior	minor	secondary

SUBSIDE	v	decline	diminish	lessen	sink
SUBSTANTIATE	v	authenticate	confirm	validate	verify
SUBTERRANEAN	a	below	beneath	buried	underground
SUBTLE	a	crafty	sly	fine	slight
SUBTLETY	n	delicacy	nicety	nuance	refinement
SUBVERT	v	overthrow	pervert	sabotage	undermine
SUCCINCT	a	brief	clear	compact	concise
SUCCUMB	v	die	surrender	submit	yield
SUFFUSE	v	fill	pervade	permeate	saturate
SUFFUSED	a	filled	flush	pervasive	saturated
SULLEN	a	gloomy	glum	moody	sulky
SUMPTUOUS	a	grand	lavish	luxurious	rich
SUPERCILIOUS	a	arrogant	contemptuous	haughty	scornful
SUPERFICIAL	a	frivolous	shallow	surface	trivial
SUPERFLUOUS	a	excessive	overabundant	surplus	unnecessary
SUPERLATIVE	a	excellent	matchless	superb	superior
SUPPLENESS	n	elasticity	flexibility	limberness	pliability
SUPPRESS	v	repress	restrain	stifle	subdue
SUPREMACY	n	authority	excellence	mastery	superiority
SURFEIT	v	cram	fill	gorge	stuff
SURFEITED	a	full	glutted	gorged	satiated
SURMISE	v	assume	guess	presume	suppose
SURPASS	v	beat	exceed	excel	outdo
SURPASSING	a	exceeding	excellent	exceptional	superior
SURREPTITIOUS	a	crafty	secretive	sneaky	underhand
SUSTENANCE	n	food	nourishment	subsistence	support
SWINDLE	v	cheat	con	defraud	trick
SYCOPHANT	n	flatterer	fawner	parasite	yes-man
SYMMETRICAL	a	balanced	harmonious	regular	uniform
SYMMETRY	n	balance	harmony	proportion	unity
SYNCHRONIZE	v	coincide	coordinate	harmonize	match
SYNOPSIS	n	digest	recap	outline	summary
SYNTAX	n	conjugation	grammar	language	sentence structure
SYNTHESIS	n	combination	fusion	integration	union
SYSTEMATIC	a	methodical	orderly	organized	regular
TACIT	a	implied	silent	unsaid	unspoken
TACITURN	a	reserved	silent	speechless	withdrawn
TACTFUL	a	considerate	diplomatic	discreet	sensitive
TAINT	v	contaminate	defile	pollute	tarnish
TAMPER	v	disturb	fiddle	interfere	meddle
TANGENTIAL	a	digressive	divergent	extraneous	peripheral
TANGIBLE	a	concrete	material	real	touchable
TANTALIZING	a	alluring	appealing	inviting	tempting

TANTAMOUNT	a	alike	equal	equivalent	same
TAPER	n	candle	light	long	slender
TARDINESS	n	idleness	lateness	slothfulness	slowness
TATTERED	a	ragged	seedy	shabby	threadbare
TAUNT	v	jeer	mock	ridicule	tease
TAWDRY	a	cheap	flashy	gaudy	showy
TEDIOUS	a	boring	dull	tiresome	uninteresting
TELLTALE	a	denotative	indicative	reflective	significant
TEMPER	v	moderate	soften	harden	toughen
TEMPERAMENT		character	disposition	nature	tendency
TEMPERATE	a	calm	composed	moderate	sober
TEMPESTUOUS	a	agitated	furious	stormy	turbulent
TENACIOUS	a	determined	firm	persistent	tough
TENET	n	belief	doctrine	opinion	principle
TENTATIVE	a	provisional	temporary	hesitant	undecided
TENURE	n	hitch	stint	term	tour
TERMINATE	v	cease	conclude	end	stop
TERRESTRIAL	a	earthly	secular	temporal	worldly
TERSE	a	abrupt	blunt	brief	curt
TESTIMONY	n	affirmation	confirmation	evidence	proof
THEOLOGIAN	n	ecclesiastic	priest	scholastic	studier of religion
THEORETICAL	a	academic	conceptual	hypothetical	speculative
THESIS	n	assumption	dissertation	proposition	theme
THREADBARE	a	ragged	seedy	shabby	tattered
THRONG	n	crowd	flock	mob	swarm
TIMOROUS	a	apprehensive	cowardly	fearful	shy
TIRADE	n	harsh	lecture	sermon	speech
TOADY	n	bootlicker	flatterer	flunky	yes-man
TOME	n	book	publication	volume	work
TORPID	a	dull	inactive	lazy	sluggish
TORPOR	n	dull	laziness	sloth	sluggishness
TORRID	a	burning	fiery	hot	scorching
TOXIC	a	deadly	harmful	poisonous	venomous
TRACT	n	area	region	essay	pamphlet
TRADITIONAL	a	common	conventional	customary	usual
TRAITOR	n	betrayer	deserter	renegade	turncoat
TRANQUIL	a	calm	peaceful	quiet	serene
TRANQUILITY	n	calm	peacefulness	quiet	serenity
TRANSCENDENT	a	abstract	idea	divine	supreme
TRANSCRIBE	v	copy	duplicate	record	reproduce
TRANSGRESSION	n	crime	offense	sin	trespass
TRANSLUCENT	a	clear	crystalline	see-through	transparent
TRAUMATIC	a	alarming	distressing	harrowing	painful

TREATISE	n	book	discourse	disquisition	dissertation
TREPIDATION	n	apprehension	dread	fear	fright
TRITE	a	clichéd	commonplace	stale	stereotyped
TRIVIAL	a	little	insignificant	trifling	unimportant
TROUPE	n	company	gang	group	team
TRUANT	n	absent	fugitive	no-show	runaway
TRUNCATE	v	abbreviate	abridge	condense	shorten
TUMULT	n	commotion	disturbance	fuss	turmoil
TUMULTUOUS	a	disorderly	stormy	tempestuous	turbulent
TURRET	n	belfry	spire	steeple	tower
TYRANNIZE	v	bully	dominate	intimidate	oppress
UBIQUITOUS	a	common	omnipresent	prevalent	universal
ULTIMATE	a	extreme	final	last	terminal
UNABRIDGED	a	complete	entire	unabbreviated	uncut
UNANIMITY	n	accord	agreement	consensus	unity
UNANIMOUS	a	agreeable	compatible	harmonious	united
UNBIASED	a	fair	impartial	just	objective
UNBLEMISHED	a	immaculate	perfect	pure	spotless
UNCANNY	a	eerie	mysterious	strange	weird
UNCONVENTIONAL	a	bizarre	eccentric	strange	unusual
UNDAUNTED	a	brave	bold	courageous	fearless
UNDERMINE	v	impair	sabotage	sap	weaken
UNDERSCORE	v	accentuate	emphasize	stress	underline
UNDERSTATEMENT	n	minimization	subtlety	trivialization	underemphasis
UNENLIGHTENED	a	ignorant	naive	uneducated	uniformed
UNETHICAL	a	crooked	dishonest	immoral	unprincipled
UNFATHOMABLE	a	deep	infinite	mysterious	puzzling
UNHERALDED	a	unannounced	unanticipated	unexpected	unpredicted
UNIFORM	a	consistent	even	regular	unchanging
MYSTERIOUS	a	cryptic	enigmatic	obscure	puzzling
UNKEMPT	a	messy	sloppy	slovenly	untidy
UNNERVING	a	alarming	creepy	disturbing	frightening
UNORTHODOX	a	peculiar	uncommon	unconventional	unusual
UNPRECEDENTED	a	new	novel	unique	unparalleled
UNREMITTING	a	constant	continuous	persistent	unceasing
UNRESTRAINED	a	free	uncontrolled	uninhibited	wild
UNSAVORY	a	disagreeable	distasteful	offensive	unpleasant
UNSCATHED	a	unharmed	unhurt	uninjured	whole
UNSEEMLY	a	improper	inappropriate	indecent	unbecoming
UNSETTLING	a	disturbing	troubling	upsetting	worrisome
UNSOUND	a	defective	faulty	invalid	weak
UNWIELDY	a	awkward	clumsy	cumbersome	ungainly
UNWITTING	a	ignorant	oblivious	unconscious	unintentional

UPBRAID	v	criticize	rebuke	reprimand	reprove
UPRIGHT	a	ethical	honest	moral	righteous
URBANE	a	refined	polished	sophisticated	worldly
USURP	v	confiscate	grab	seize	take over
UTILITY	n	advantage	benefit	service	usefulness
VACILLATE	v	fluctuate	hesitate	stagger	waver
VACILLATION	n	fluctuation	hesitation	uncertainty	wavering
VAGARY	n	fancy	notion	quirk	whim
VAGUE	a	hazy	indefinite	indistinct	unclear
VALEDICTORY	a	departing	farewell	last	parting
VALID	a	authentic	legitimate	sound	true
VALIDATE	v	authenticate	certify	confirm	verify
VALOR	n	boldness	bravery	courage	heroism
VANDALISM	n	desolation	destruction	devastation	hooliganism
VANE	n	blade	weathercock	weather vane	wind vane
VANQUISH	v	beat	conquer	defeat	overcome
VANTAGE POINT	n	angle	perspective	position	viewpoint
VEGETATION	n	botany	flora	growth	plants
VEHEMENT	a	fierce	intense	urgent	violent
VEILED	a	concealed	covered	hidden	obscure
VENERABLE	a	aged	old	respected	revered
VENGEFUL	a	hostile	retaliatory	revengeful	spiteful
VENT	v	air	discharge	outlet	release
VERBOSE	a	talkative	long-winded	windy	wordy
VERBOSITY	n	talkativeness	long-windedness	windiness	wordiness
VERIFIABLE	a	certain	confirmable	demonstrable	true
VERIFY	v	authenticate	confirm	prove	validate
VERITABLE	a	authentic	genuine	real	true
VERNACULAR	n	common	dialect	informal	slang
VERSATILE	a	adaptable	dexterous	flexible	variable
VEXATIOUS	a	annoying	irksome	irritating	troublesome
VIBRANT	a	active	energetic	lively	resounding
VIGILANT	a	alert	attentive	cautious	watchful
VIGOR	n	energy	force	power	strength
VIGOROUS	a	active	energetic	lively	strong
VILIFY	v	attack	defame	disparage	slander
VIOLATE	v	defile	disobey	infringe	transgress
VIRTUALLY	a	almost	nearly	practically	substantially
VIRTUE	n	excellence	goodness	merit	quality
VIRTUOSO	n	ace	expert	genius	master
VIRTUOUS	a	honest	moral	pure	righteous
VIRULENT	a	deadly	malignant	poisonous	venomous
VISCERAL	a	instinctive	internal	intuitive	unreasoning

122

VITAL	a	critical	essential	important	necessary
VITALITY	n	animation	energy	life	spirit
VIVACIOUS	a	active	animated	lively	spirited
VIVID	a	brilliant	bright	clear	graphic
VOCIFEROUS	a	boisterous	clamorous	loud	noisy
VOID	a	barren	clear	empty	vacant
VOID	v	annul	cancel	quash	vacate
VOLATILE	a	changeable	fickle	flighty	unstable
VOLITION	n	choice	decision	determination	will
VOLUMINOUS	a	extensive	great	large	massive
VOLUNTARY	a	free	intentional	spontaneous	willful
VORACIOUS	a	greedy	hungry	insatiable	piggish
VULGAR	a	coarse	crude	indecent	rude
VULNERABLE	a	exposed	susceptible	unprotected	weak
WALLOW	v	delight	indulge	flounder	roll
WANE	v	decline	decrease	dissipate	wither
WANTON	a	abandoned	immoral	loose	promiscuous
WARINESS	n	alertness	caution	prudence	vigilance
WARY	a	alert	careful	cautious	watchful
WAYWARD	a	contrary	disobedient	perverse	unruly
WEATHERED	a	battered	beaten	seasoned	worn
WHARF	n	berth	dock	landing	pier
WHIM	n	fancy	impulse	notion	quirk
WHIMSICAL	a	erratic	fanciful	fantastic	fickle
WHOLESOME	a	beneficial	fit	good	healthy
WILLFUL	a	deliberate	insistent	headstrong	obstinate
WILY	a	crafty	cunning	shrewd	sly
WINSOME	a	attractive	charming	engaging	winning
WITTY	a	amusing	clever	funny	humorous
WREAK	v	cause	exact	impose	inflict
WRITHE	v	agonize	squirm	twist	wriggle
WRY	a	askew	crooked	lopsided	twisted
YEARNINGS	n	cravings	desires	hungers	longings
ZEAL	n	eagerness	earnestness	enthusiasm	passion
ZEALOUS	a	devoted	eager	enthusiastic	passionate

BIOGRAPHY

Dr. McClerren's undergraduate studies began in Education, his graduate studies in Counseling, Adult and Higher Education, culminating with an RsD in 1016.

Dr. McClerren is a committed life long learner: a 21st century Renaissance man. Among his accomplishments are those of private pilot, missile technician and award winning vocal musician.

Dr. McClerren has been a certified teacher in Illinois since 1977. He has taught for San Diego City College, ITT Technical Institute and the University of Oklahoma.

Dr. McClerren's experience in academic advisement includes both high school students and military personnel. His work in the field began in 2003 as an Education Advisor for the Navy College Program.

Dr. McClerren is also Licensed Local Pastor of the United Methodist Church in Chicago. He is married; and lives with his wife and daughter in Lake County Illinois.